MY POCKET
meditations

ANYTIME EXERCISES FOR
PEACE, CLARITY, AND FOCUS

MEERA LESTER

ADAMS MEDIA
NEW YORK   LONDON   TORONTO   SYDNEY   NEW DELHI

Adams Media
An Imprint of Simon & Schuster, Inc.
57 Littlefield Street
Avon, Massachusetts 02322

First Adams Media trade paperback edition AUGUST 2017

ADAMS MEDIA and colophon are trademarks of Simon and Schuster.

For information about special discounts for bulk purchases, please contact Simon & Schuster Special Sales at 1-866-506-1949 or business@simonandschuster.com.

The Simon & Schuster Speakers Bureau can bring authors to your live event. For more information or to book an event contact the Simon & Schuster Speakers Bureau at 1-866-248-3049 or visit our website at www.simonspeakers.com.

Interior images © iStockphoto.com/hpkalyani

Manufactured in China

10 9 8 7 6 5 4 3 2 1

Library of Congress Cataloging-in-Publication Data has been applied for.

ISBN 978-1-5072-0341-5
ISBN 978-1-5072-0342-2 (ebook)

CONTENTS

Introduction   9

MEDITATIONS ON PEACE **17**

meditation 1:   Quiet Mind, Open Heart   18

meditation 2:   The Serene Mind Engenders Joy   19

meditation 3:   Peaceful Coexistence with the Earth   20

meditation 4:   A Walking Meditation on Peace   21

meditation 5:   Be the Peaceful Warrior   22

meditation 6:   Shift the Fire in the Belly to a Peaceful Pose . .   23

meditation 7:   Thread the Necklace of Prayer Beads
                and Chant   24

meditation 8:   Yoga for Peaceful Sleep   25

meditation 9:   Transmit Love and Peace to Those Who've
                Passed On   26

meditation 10: Do the Ancient So'Ham Chant for Peace   27

meditation 11: Relinquish Worry to a Higher Power   28

meditation 12: Singing Bowl to Soothe the Spirit   29

MEDITATIONS ON INTENTION AND WILLPOWER **31**

meditation 1:   Relinquish the Need to Control   32

meditation 2:   Virtuous Will versus Willfulness   33

meditation 3:   Redirect Emotion Using Intention   35

meditation 4:   View a Visual Image of Willpower   36

meditation 5:   A New Habit Begins with Intention
                and Resolve   37

meditation 6: Use Intention to Manifest Something Desired 38

meditation 7: Grow a Stronger Backbone Through Willpower 39

meditation 8: Use Intention to Discover Your Life's Purpose 40

meditation 9: Align Your Will with Works to Benefit the Earth. 42

meditation 10: Letting Go of Hindrances 43

MEDITATIONS ON SYNCHRONICITY **45**

meditation 1: The Doorway to the Infinite 46

meditation 2: Look for Linkage in Meaningful Coincidences . 47

meditation 3: The Power of Infinite Possibility 48

meditation 4: Note Synchronous Guideposts. 49

meditation 5: Synchronicity and the Law of Unity 50

meditation 6: The Energy of Gratitude. 51

meditation 7: Declutter to Recognize Synchronous Events. . 52

meditation 8: Mine Your Dreams for Meaningful Coincidences 54

meditation 9: The Universe Speaks, You Notice 55

meditation 10: Find Meaning in Synchronous Events 56

MEDITATIONS ON FRIENDSHIP **57**

meditation 1: Open Heart, Hand of Friendship. 58

meditation 2: Cultivate the Qualities of the Divine. 59

meditation 3: Be Mindful of the Other in Your Friendship . . 60

meditation 4: Be a Friend to the Earth. 61

meditation 5: Be a Compassionate Friend to All Creatures. . 62

meditation 6: Where You See Darkness, Shine a Light 63

meditation 7: Treasure Spiritual Friends. 64

meditation 8: Heart-Centered Love for Man's Best Friend . . 65

meditation 9: Find Friends in Other Cultures 66

meditation 10: Be Friends to Those Less Fortunate 67

MEDITATIONS ON LOVE AND COMPASSION 69

meditation 1: Breathing a Circle of Love 70

meditation 2: Gifts of the Red Lotus 71

meditation 3: The Prayer Wheel Mantra 72

meditation 4: Loving-Kindness Meditation 73

meditation 5: Love and Knot Knowing 74

meditation 6: Show Yourself a Little Tenderness 75

meditation 7: Aromatherapy Stimulates Love Energy 76

meditation 8: Love by Any Other Name 77

meditation 9: Season Your Life with Love for Real Success . . 78

meditation 10: Love Your Cause 79

MEDITATIONS ON GRATITUDE 81

meditation 1: Relive a Walk in the Woods 82

meditation 2: Journal Your Gratitude 83

meditation 3: Use the Language of Gratitude 84

meditation 4: Mentor, Lover, Stranger, Friend 85

meditation 5: Practice Gratitude 86

meditation 6: The Earth Blesses You, You Bless the Earth . . 87

meditation 7: Honor Your Dynamic Imagination 88

meditation 8: Gratitude for Veterans and Wounded
Warriors 89

meditation 9: A World of Humanitarian Work 90

meditation 10: Gratitude for Courage During
Unspeakable Loss 91

MEDITATIONS ON FORGIVENESS AND MERCY 93

MEDITATION 1: Don't Sweat the Small Stuff. 94

MEDITATION 2: The Way to Forgiveness. 95

MEDITATION 3: Seek Self-Mercy in the Landscape of Being . . 96

MEDITATION 4: Apology and Forgiveness. 98

MEDITATION 5: Shifting the Paradigm 100

MEDITATION 6: Meditation for Those in Distress. 101

MEDITATION 7: Tap Into Your Inner Kuan Yin 102

MEDITATION 8: Nowhere to Hide. 103

MEDITATION 9: Works of Mercy, Compassion in Action. 104

MEDITATIONS ON SACRIFICE 105

MEDITATION 1: Sacrifice for the Greater Good. 106

MEDITATION 2: Altruism, Empathy, and Sacrifice. 107

MEDITATION 3: Sacrifices Change the World 108

MEDITATION 4: Life Changes Require Sacrifices 109

MEDITATION 5: How to Know When You Are Sacrificing
Too Much 110

MEDITATION 6: The Call to Sacrifice Is a Gift 111

MEDITATION 7: Sacrifice the Lies of Your Ego. 112

MEDITATION 8: The Shelter of Community 113

MEDITATION 9: The Circle of Seasonal Sacrifices. 114

MEDITATIONS ON HUMILITY 115

MEDITATION 1: Cultivating Humility 116

MEDITATION 2: The Symbolic Color of Humility 117

MEDITATION 3: Humility on the Job 118

MEDITATION 4: Signs of Humility 119

MEDITATION 5: The Medieval View of Humility 120

MEDITATION 6: Give Competitors Their Due   121

MEDITATION 7: What Foot Washing Teaches 122

MEDITATION 8: The Humble Pranama 123

MEDITATION 9: Praise All the Good That You Find 124

MEDITATIONS ON HOPE 125

MEDITATION 1: Finding Hope in a New Day 126

MEDITATION 2: The Soothing Balm of Hope 127

MEDITATION 3: The Inner Wellspring of Hope Heals 128

MEDITATION 4: Hope for Change 129

MEDITATION 5: Hope for a Stable and Peaceful World 130

MEDITATION 6: A Powerful Elixir for Renewal   131

MEDITATION 7: Confident Expectation in Crisis 132

MEDITATION 8: Hope for the Long Visit 134

MEDITATION 9: Hold on to Your Hopes and Dreams 135

MEDITATIONS ON JUSTICE 137

MEDITATION 1: Mindfulness for Social and Cultural Justice . . 138

MEDITATION 2: Karmic Justice 139

MEDITATION 3: The Tarot's Justice Card 140

MEDITATION 4: Distributive Justice   141

MEDITATION 5: Justice and Moral Law 143

MEDITATION 6: Ahimsa in Times of Injustice 144

MEDITATION 7: Social Justice—Serving from the Inside Out . . 145

MEDITATION 8: Safeguarding Women's Rights 146

MEDITATION 9: Activism and Justice for Animal Rights 147

MEDITATIONS ON BIRTH AND DEATH **149**

meditation 1: Why Wait to Contact the Divine? 150

meditation 2: The Doorway to the Beyond 151

meditation 3: The Cessation of Breath Also Symbolizes
Birth 152

meditation 4: Past-Life Regression As a Healing Modality . . 153

meditation 5: Mental Impulse Informs the Desire to
Create Stuff 155

meditation 6: Thousands of Sparks 156

meditation 7: Tap Into the Regenerative Power of Scorpio . . 157

meditation 8: Heal Old Wounds to Generate Renewal 158

meditation 9: Subdue Your Mind Waves 159

MEDITATIONS ON PRESENCE **161**

meditation 1: Notice the Presences in Your Life 162

meditation 2: Let Music Lift You Into Sacred Presence 163

meditation 3: Kindle the Lights 164

meditation 4: Use Imagery to Find Presence 165

meditation 5: Find Ancient Presence in Centuries-Old
Sanctuaries 166

meditation 6: The Landscape of Longing 167

meditation 7: Remembering the Presence of Ancestors . . . 168

meditation 8: Sit with a Tree 169

meditation 9: The Memory of Place 170

Index 171

INTRODUCTION

"Life is a series of spontaneous changes.
Don't resist them—that only creates sorrow. Let reality be reality.
Let things flow naturally forward in whatever way they like."

—Lao Tzu, sixth-century B.C.E. founder of Taoism

Living a balanced life in the modern era can be challenging. Not only must we keep our hectic—often stressful—daily schedules of work and family activities, but we must also take care of our bodies and emotional well-being. What about our spiritual welfare?

Yoga, meditation, positive thinking, and adhering to a spiritual practice such as one of the various paths of Buddhism can transform your life. Not only do these practices bestow healthful benefits and stress-busting strategies for re-establishing balance, but you can also discover your true nature and experience enlightenment. Even if you can spare only a few minutes each day to unyoke your mind from worldly cares to turn inward, you will begin to experience the meditation benefits that include:

* Developing and enhancing your intuition.
* Gaining insight into reality versus illusion.
* Staying calm in any situation.
* Having better health and enjoyment of life.
* Letting go of cravings and attachments to all things unstable and impermanent.

To live, grow older, and evolve is to encounter change. It's a certainty. Life is dynamic, not static, and change—properly viewed—can be a wonderful thing, pushing us in new directions and challenging us in new ways. Buddhist monk Thich Nhat Hanh noted, "We have more possibilities available in each moment than we think."

The allure of the dazzling and seductive cosmic dance of life exerts a strong pull on us through our senses. But we can also take our leave from witnessing and participating in this dance when we desire a centered, peaceful grounding. The ancient practice of meditation offers a harbor of serenity and the means to restore balance and equilibrium in mind, body, and spirit. The wisdom keepers of the world's great spiritual traditions like Lao Tzu, Christ, and the Buddha understood this truth.

Guided meditations make it easier to shepherd the restless mind toward a single focal point like the breath, an energy center or chakra, a ritual position of the hands or another part of the body, or a sacred object or image. The point is to quiet the mind in order to be fully aware. For some, meditative practice is the means to explore the sacred mystical forces underpinning life. Others seek the benefits of better health, mental acuity, and emotional well-being. Regardless of why you practice meditation, the goal is to still the ever-chattering mind. Those who take the time to meditate will reap the rewards.

HEALTH BENEFITS OF MEDITATION

Inducing deep relaxation during meditation facilitates profound changes in your body, including reducing stress hormone levels. Meditation also decreases the respiratory and pulse rates as well as lowers blood pressure for a positive impact on cardiovascular health. Studies have shown that daily meditation can alter your mood nearly as effectively as antidepressant medication. It can also stimulate creativity, strengthen the immune system, and reduce anxiety associated with pain.

Stick with a meditation regimen to discover a lighter mood and a happier disposition. Studies of long-term meditators by the medical profession have shown that the deeply relaxed state of mind that happens in meditation triggers a release by the brain of dopamine, serotonin, oxytocin, and endorphins—the "feel good" neurotransmitters linked to diverse aspects of happiness.

If you are the type of individual who'd rather walk than sit, a moving meditation might be right for you. During a walking meditation, you'll synchronize your breath with your steps for an experience of mindfulness in each moment. Prayerful, meditative walking is an ancient practice that has found expression in various spiritual traditions. There is no right or wrong way to do a walking meditation—simply be receptive, relaxed, and aware. The beauty of a walking meditation is twofold: You gain the benefits of both exercise and meditation.

SPIRITUAL ASPECTS OF MEDITATION

The twin gifts of physical and mental well-being may be enough to inspire some to take up meditation, but others are attracted to the deeper insights into the subtle realms of the spirit. Spiritual yearning dates back to the earliest days of humankind. The practice of meditation to discover the meaning and purpose of life is found in spiritual and philosophical movements and belief systems throughout the world. A one-pointed focus, steady awareness, and deep, slow breathing can balance the threefold construct of body, brain, and environment, returning your experience of the world to a more neutral, peaceful state.

EASTERN TRADITION YOGA MEDITATION

Though some in the West might associate yoga with a collection of physical exercises that include strengthening stretches and postures absent a spiritual, religious, or philosophical component, the same is not true for the East, where yoga originated. Traditional hatha yoga, as practiced in Eastern wisdom traditions, has meditation at its heart. In Tibet, India, Bhutan, Nepal, and elsewhere in the East, yoga and meditation along with *pranayama* (breath control) and *mudras* (ritual gestures) are often integral aspects of an individual's *sadhana* (personal spiritual practice).

The oldest text on hatha yoga—*Hatha Yoga Pradipika*, composed in the fifteenth century by Swami Swatmarama—covers poses and yogic breathing techniques as well as symbolic ritual gestures of the hands (mudras) seen in Hindu and Buddhist spiritual imagery. The praying hands position, where the palms touch and the fingers point straight up, is a well-known mudra. Accompanied by the word *namaste*, it becomes a respectful greeting. In spiritual traditions such as Buddhism and Hinduism, hatha yoga practice includes poses, meditation, pranayama (breath control), and mudras to lock, stimulate, and redirect subtle energy along pathways to and from the chakras.

THE CHAKRAS

The word "chakra" comes from the Sanskrit word for "wheel." In the philosophies of Buddhism and Hinduism, these wheels or energy centers are points where the psychic energy of the subtle (or energy) body interacts with areas of the physical body. There are seven main chakras (vortices of energy) in the subtle body that affect the mind-body system. They line up in the subtle body along the spine at intervals that correspond to specific areas of the physical body. Chakras are the sites where the energies of the body and consciousness converge; moreover, each chakra has a unique vibration.

The energy of the chakras flows through subtle channels called *nadis* ("*nad*" means movement). Ayurveda, an ancient healing system that originated in India more than 3,000 years ago, makes mention of 70,000 nadis. A fundamental concept in Ayurveda relates to the life force with which the nadis and chakra energies at optimum are always aligned. When they are open, moving, and flowing they create a strong life force; when they are blocked they create stagnation, obstacles, and a weak life force.

The chakras are also associated with specific sounds, colors, and powers. The seven chakras are:

* **Muladhara** (the root chakra). The inner sound is Lam; the color is red. Root chakra energy heightens the sense of smell and bolsters physical strength. Here is where you experience the fight-or-flight response.
* **Svadhisthana** (the sacral chakra, located above the pubic bone). The inner sound is Vam; the color is orange. Sacral chakra energy intensifies your sense of taste and stimulates creativity.
* **Manipura** (situated at the solar plexus). The inner sound is Ram; the color is yellow. This chakra enhances the sense of sight, increases vitality, and strengthens personal power.
* **Anahata** (situated at the heart center). The inner sound is Yam; the color is green. This chakra is the source of love. Its energy magnifies the sense of touch and increases the expression of compassion.
* **Vishuddha** (located in the throat area). The inner sound is Ham; the color is blue. This chakra is associated with verbal expression, trust, and loyalty. Throat chakra energy intensifies the sense of sound and fosters courage.
* **Ajna** (found at the point between the eyebrows, or spiritual third-eye center). The inner sound is *AUM*; the color is indigo. Its energy enhances imagination, psychic abilities, and inspired thought.
* **Sahasrara** (positioned at the crown of the head). The inner sound is Ham; the color is violet. Referred to as the thousand-petal lotus flower, this chakra is associated with enlightenment and

connection to the Infinite Intelligence. The crown chakra intensifies your knowingness/wisdom and connection to God.

THE BREATH IN MEDITATION

With yoga and meditation, breath becomes an important tool—its movement is rising, falling, or retained. The modern practice of yoga draws upon the ancient teachings and practices of pranayama. By observing the cycle of the incoming and outgoing breaths, the incessant chatter of the mind slows. A simple conscious breathing (pranayama) technique is to count the breaths. An old yogic teaching is to sequentially attach a name of God to the inflowing breath and a number to the exhaled breath.

Various other breathing techniques have become popular—some used in conjunction with yoga asanas, or stretching/resting poses, and meditation. Other breath work for spiritual work or health focuses on redirecting the flow of energies to awaken the dormant primal energy (kundalini). This energy, coiled at the base of the spine (where the Ida and Pingala channels lie along its left and right sides, respectively), was identified long before the fifteenth century, when it became associated with hatha yoga. By the sixteenth century, the term *kundalini* came into wider use, appearing in a series of texts written on the meditations and yoga methodologies known as the Yoga Upanishads.

When this energy rises in the central channel along the spine (the Sushumna) to reach the crown chakra, the result is enlightenment. The yogi or yogini attains mystical gifts: truth, consciousness, and bliss, or to use the Sanskrit terms, *sat-chit-ananda*. For this reason, many schools of yoga stress the importance of this awakening through meditation, mantra chanting of sacred sounds or words, pranayama, and yoga practice. Kundalini yoga practitioners have described a typical physical sensation of an electrical current moving along the back from the tailbone to the head.

A few pranayama practices involve holding the breath for a particular interval, but these should be undertaken only with the supervision of a qualified instructor and not attempted by individuals with heart ailments, blood pressure issues, or breathing problems, such as asthma. Otherwise, conscious breathing is excellent for proper oxygenation and relaxing the body as it prepares for deep meditation or sleep.

Some types of pranayama include:

* **Complete Breath** (observing the complete filling and emptying of the lungs with air)
* **Universal Healing Mantra** (So'Ham or Anapana Sati; mindfulness of movement of the breath in your body)
* **Alternate Nostril Breathing** (Nadi Shodhana; controlling which nostril the breath flows through)
* **Bollows Breath** (Dastrika, rapid breathing)
* **Psychic Breath or Cobra Breath** (Ujjayi; moving the body through one yogic pose to the next either on inhalation or on exhalation)
* **Bee Breath** (Brahmari; breathing with eyes closed and ears plugged and listening in the head to the humming sound created during exhalation from the throat)

MUSIC IN MEDITATION

The language of music speaks directly to the soul, regardless of the nationality, race, or gender of the individual creating or listening to the sound. The singing of devotional songs, hymns, or chants is a practice found in all religious and spiritual traditions. Such music elevates mood and consciousness and energetically charges the atmosphere. Sacred sounds draw the mind inward.

In Buddhism, the ringing of a bell serves as an invocation to sit in meditation. In the Hindu tradition, the ringing of bells beckons the faithful to meditate, while reminding devotees that the Divine is present in the world. In the Judeo-Christian tradition, liturgical music (sung and played on instruments) lifts the heart and spirit, while pealing bells commonly summon the faithful to church and a tinkling bell may be used to begin or end a ritual. This musical summoning finds resonance in the *adhan*, or Islamic call to prayer, albeit through the human voice. A singing bowl serves as the quintessential tool to beckon Tibetan Buddhist monks to enter deep meditation. From this ancient Buddhist culture come monks who have mastered a type of guttural chant referred to as "throat singing."

Perhaps the simplest method of making music includes sticks tapping and hands clapping. Such music may be devotional, leading the mind inward and opening the heart. Modern science reveals that when listening to or joining in the making of sacred music, changes happen in our bodies on a cellular level.

Sacred sounds open your heart and draw you inward. Revered Buddhist monk Thich Nhat Hanh noted that every time a bell rings in his community, he and his followers stop where they are and stop what they are doing to turn inward—away from thinking, conversations, and work—to focus on mindful breathing. The point is to return to the Self. Over time, your spiritual perceptions become altered, your insight evolves, and your wisdom deepens. Meditation reveals the richness of life while guiding you toward the truth of who you are, giving you a glimpse of self-realization. This sea change can take place over a lifetime or happen in an instant. But this self-knowing is your ultimate task in life—your dharma—and meditation is the way.

MEDITATIONS
ON PEACE

Peace is the universally recognized state of stillness and calm. The ancient Sanskrit word for peace is *shanti*. Reciting this beautiful word at the end a period of prayer or meditation aligns your clear and quiet thoughts with your peaceful being. As you step back into life, you convey and transmit peace to others in a silent blessing.

QUIET MIND, OPEN HEART

First attempts to sit in meditation can be frustrating. You can quiet your body, but your thoughts dance on. Let them. If you watch your thoughts without directing or interfering with them—what Lao Tzu, father of Taoism, called *wu-wei*, or non-doing—your thoughts will slow. When you rest in awareness with an open heart, you will begin to sense the ancient, quiet wellspring from which inner peace flows.

1. Wear loose, comfortable clothes. Remove your shoes as well as jewelry, ties, and belts that bind.
2. Choose a comfortable sitting position. Support your buttocks with pillows, if necessary.
3. Straighten your spine. Rest open palms on your thighs. If you tend to feel chilly, place a soft throw around your shoulders and over your lap. Forget the body.
4. Close your eyes. Take a couple of cleansing breaths and then breathe in and out in a slow rhythm. Relax. Mentally let go of thoughts about your external environment. Let your heart be open and receptive.
5. Imagine your mind is a mountain lake. Your restless thoughts are ripples pushed by an airstream across the surface. When the breezes stop, the lake becomes still. Imagine the lake's surface reflecting the full moon; its light is the Divine source of calm and well-being. Absorb the calm. Let peaceful awareness permeate your being.

THE SERENE MIND ENGENDERS JOY

The inwardly turned mind that is not asleep, not thinking, and yet alert produces physiological changes in the body. Slower breathing drives down blood pressure and heart rate. As your oxygen consumption goes down, your mind—in a state of relaxed awareness—begins to behold itself and experience joy. This is the foundation for the meditation and contemplation practiced by saints and sages over time throughout the world. This meditation brings a joyful peace. As the Buddha notes, "Joy follows a pure thought like a shadow that never leaves."

1. With eyes closed, direct your attention to the space between your brows. This will be your focal point for this meditation. Gently gaze into that space without straining.
2. As thoughts or emotions arise to threaten your peace, don't try to reason, deny, or argue them away. That would be conflicting and counterproductive, derailing your meditation. Don't be hard on yourself but rather practice patience and loving-kindness. Maintain a detached awareness of what arises during meditation.
3. In Buddhism, inner peace isn't a static condition. It is a dynamic state brimming with insight, perception, knowledge, and compassion.
4. Hold on to the awareness of that inner peace. Carry that joyful serenity unhindered into your day.

PEACEFUL COEXISTENCE WITH THE EARTH

Many Eastern philosophies, including nature-based spiritual paths, embrace the idea of showing kindness to all living beings, nature, and planet earth. To access the full benefit of earth's peaceful and healing energies, do this meditation lying on your back on a yoga mat or a folded blanket on the ground.

1. Lie on your back with a long spine and with your legs straight out and your arms resting at your sides (Corpse Pose).
2. Mentally surrender to the Divine Power that created the earth and all life forms and organisms that dwell upon it.
3. Breathe in and visualize waves of peaceful energies flowing into your spine and radiating out to all parts of your body, spreading peace and healing energies along every meridian and into every cell.
4. Breathe out, feeling gratitude while visualizing the return of the waves of energy to their source—Mother Earth.

Embrace Nonviolence

To honor and engage in a peaceful coexistence with the earth, there are many things each individual can do. These include embracing nonviolence toward the earth as well as recycling, restoring, preserving, and revering the earth and the life it supports.

A WALKING MEDITATION ON PEACE

This simple mindfulness practice with a focus on peace can be directed toward loved ones, coworkers, friends, associates, adversaries, or our planet earth. It requires no special preparation beyond clearing your mind of negative thoughts in order to experience the awe-inspiring beauty of nature while practicing mindfulness in each moment. Buddhist monk Thich Nhat Hanh counsels, "Smile, breathe, and go slowly."

1. Choose a place for a quiet walk in nature—perhaps across a meadow, around a lake, into the mountains or desert, or through a garden.
2. Tread softly. Open your heart. Surrender to the blessings of all that is good and beautiful in each moment.
3. Notice the peace in your environment, how nature synthesizes opposites in a harmonious way.
4. Maintain a calm, present-centered awareness of your body and your feelings as you stroll.
5. As peace descends upon you like a diaphanous veil, send peace from your heart to others with the knowledge that your thoughts, intentions, and emotions are carrying the current of peace to whomever you have chosen to receive it.

BE THE PEACEFUL WARRIOR

His Holiness Tenzin Gyatso, the fourteenth Dalai Lama, said, "We can never obtain peace in the outer world until we make peace with ourselves." When conflict comes into your day and disturbs your peace, know that those moments will pass into impermanence. Bad behavior is a temporary action. Experiencing it from others requires tolerance and patience. The challenge is to become the peaceful warrior who wisely does not build a permanent construction out of something impermanent.

1. Assume the right-sided Warrior Pose, one of the most graceful of all yoga poses. It strengthens the lower back, the thighs, the arms, and the legs while bestowing grace, courage, and peace. This wide-stance pose has the right foot in a forward position while the left foot is a shoulder-width behind and perpendicular to the right. The left hand rests on the left thigh as the right hand stretches upward as if reaching for the sun like a mighty warrior.

2. Breathe out. With tenderness and gentleness, push your pelvis down and hold the posture as would a peaceful warrior. Smile with sincerity. Continue breathing out as you descend.

3. Breathing in, come up. Then, breathe out as you lower your hands to your sides and repeat the posture on your left side.

4. Release any tension the body is holding with the exhaled breath. Feel the balance. Feel the strength. Notice the stamina and balance in your body. Feel how strong yet peaceful each part of your body has become.

5. Realize that this is the peaceful strength embraced by the Shaolin warriors.

SHIFT THE FIRE IN THE BELLY TO A PEACEFUL POSE

To restore equilibrium when you feel off balance, shift heightened levels of emotion or stress in your gut. Emotions and stress are most often held at the third-chakra level, between the belly button and the rib cage. This chakra in the subtle body is known as the Manipura chakra. Yoga poses that stimulate this chakra and strengthen your core enable you to subdue emotions, restore balance, and reclaim peace.

1. After warming up your core, stand with feet aligned with your shoulders at a distance of about a foot apart. Slightly bend your knees.
2. Press your palms together and raise your arms over your head. Think of your arms and hands working together to levy a blow, as though you are using a hatchet to open a coconut.
3. Exclaim "Ha" (the sound associated with the Manipura chakra) loudly as you heave down your arms and hands in a single, swift movement to release emotional energy. Repeat until you feel emptied and calm.
4. Move your mat to the wall. Lie supine with your legs up the wall, palms open, and eyes closed.
5. Breathe away any remaining stress until peace settles upon you.

THREAD THE NECKLACE OF PRAYER BEADS AND CHANT

For thousands of years, pilgrims of various faiths have used necklaces of prayer beads to connect the physical sense of touch with the mental practice of chanting words imbued with spiritual energy.

1. Sit in a comfortable meditation pose. Close your eyes. Hold the first bead on the string in your right hand.
2. Chant the word *AUM/OM* (sacred sound of creation) or *shanti* (peace).
3. Repeat the word as you move your fingers to the second bead, the third, and so on. When you reach the end of the string of beads, stop at that juncture, turn the string of beads around, and work your way back in the direction you started.

Holy Sound

Ancient Vedic scriptures describe *AUM* or *OM* as the totality of all sound, existence, and consciousness—the holiest of all sounds. It is an incantation that starts many prayers, sacred ceremonies, and chants. Both a symbol and a sound, *OM* and its variations such as *AUM* when chanted sound much the same. The "a-u" sound of *AUM* combine to make the "o" vowel and the "m" sound is produced with closed lips and often held three times as long as the length of time it takes to pronounce one vowel.

YOGA FOR PEACEFUL SLEEP

The intermediate state before sleep is known as the hypnagogic state. The following conscious breathing exercise, known in yoga as the Complete Breath, produces rapid relaxation and feelings of peace as it clears the mind, generates positive feelings, and repatterns thought. Try the Complete Breath technique before sleep. It can take five to fifteen minutes of this meditation to feel deeply relaxed and peaceful.

1. Lie on your back (supine position).
2. Breathe in slowly through your nose and notice the movement of the breath as it fills the lower, middle, and upper parts of your lungs as your diaphragm moves down (contracts), opening your chest (thoracic cavity).
3. Notice how the breath empties from the upper, middle, and lower areas of your lungs as you exhale.
4. Observe how your diaphragm moves up (relaxes) and the chest cavity returns to its unexpanded (closed) state.

Prime Your Dreaming Mind

To incubate a dream or ask for knowledge about something, enter the hypnagogic state and pose a question for which you would like your dreaming mind to work on the answer, so you have it when you awaken in the morning. This breathing technique relieves some of the chronic adverse effects of stress.

TRANSMIT LOVE AND PEACE TO THOSE WHO'VE PASSED ON

Wisdom traditions (both Eastern and Western) honor the dead with prayers and positive thoughts of eternal peace and tranquility. Honoring a loved one on a special day during the calendar year is also a tradition in many cultures. Paramahansa Yogananda, the founder of Self-Realization Fellowship, suggested a simple process for transmitting peaceful, loving thoughts to a loved one who has passed on.

1. Sit in a quiet room. Close your eyes and meditate on the Divine.
2. Feeling the Holy Presence, focus your inward attention on the inner eye or point between the eyebrows (known as the third eye in Buddhism and Hinduism).
3. Visualize the person you want to receive your peaceful and loving thoughts.
4. Think of your thoughts as energy vibrations that you mentally push toward that loved one.
5. Attach your outgoing vibration of love to each outgoing breath, if that helps.
6. Continue to broadcast your love, peace, and goodwill.
7. Mentally affirm to your loved one's spirit that the two of you will meet again.

> "Better than a thousand useless words is one useful word, hearing which one attains peace."
>
> —*The Dhammapada* (collection of Buddhist sayings)

DO THE ANCIENT SO'HAM CHANT FOR PEACE

Raja yoga teaches that a quiet mind is necessary to perceive the God-Self within. When you sit immobile in a comfortable yoga pose and slow your breathing cycles through the mental practice of "So'Ham," your mind becomes still and clear. Like a mirror, the peaceful mind accurately reflects the image of the true inner Self.

1. Sit cross-legged with a straight spine and palms resting up and open on your knees.
2. On each hand, join your index finger with your thumb and keep your hands relaxed. This is called Sukhasana, one of the easiest yoga poses.
3. Close your eyes and focus your attention on the point between your brows; do not strain.
4. Mentally express "So" as you draw the breath in and "Ham" as you exhale—these are the natural sounds of the breath.
5. Keep the mind's eye focused on that "third-eye" point and concentrated on the breath.
6. Notice how as concentration deepens, your breathing slows.
7. Deepen your focus.
8. Notice how peace descends upon and within you as gently as fog enshrouds a mountain.
9. Feel in your heart and soul that you are the ever-present, all-pervading, all-blissful Soul.
10. Rest in the awareness that your soul is a reflection of the ever-joyful Spirit—Peace itself.

RELINQUISH WORRY TO A HIGHER POWER

Paramahansa Yogananda asserted, "When you have peace in every movement of your body . . . thinking . . . willpower . . . love, and peace and God in your ambitions, remember—you have connected God with your life." Feeling protected and at peace is easy when you accept that you are not in control and turn over all your concern to a Higher Power. The best balm for a burdened mind is to stop fretting and settle down. Worry gives rise to a deeper delusion within you. Quiet your heart and still your mind. Use the following simple breathing technique to re-establish equilibrium in your consciousness before making your positive affirmation for protection and peace.

1. Inhale to the count of six.
2. Hold for a count of six.
3. Exhale to the count of twelve.
4. Hold the breath for a count of six.
5. Repeat these steps ten or more times and then affirm: "I am protected by the Divine, whose spirit is before me, behind me, beneath me, above me, to the left of me and the right. I have nothing to fear within or without. All is as it should be, according to Divine Will. I am at peace."

SINGING BOWL TO SOOTHE THE SPIRIT

If you want to live a healthy, happy, spiritually enlightened, and peaceful life, learn to witness without judgment. Shift your vibration to higher consciousness. Critical and judgmental thinking finds resonance in old patterns that you can reject. Become the neutral observer. If you require assistance with this practice, try a Tibetan singing bowl, used for centuries to instill a deep relaxation, balance chakras, facilitate holistic healing, and help you turn deeply within to the Self that is the image of the Divine.

1. Sit comfortably (use a cushion if necessary) with your spine erect and shoulders level.
2. In one hand hold the bowl on your relaxed, extended fingertips (if the bowl is small) or on your palm with fingers spread evenly apart.
3. Tip the bowl toward your other arm as though you were about to whisk some batter in it.
4. Using your free hand, grasp the mallet, placing the fingers about halfway down.
5. Gently tap the bowl and tune in to the sound and vibration.
6. Holding the mallet straight up and down against the outside edge of the rim of the bowl and using your whole arm (not just the wrist), apply pressure as you guide the mallet around the lip of the bowl in a clockwise motion.
7. For a deeper sound, use the same clockwise motion around the outer middle of the bowl rather than the rim.
8. Enjoy the clear sounds and deeper tones and let peace vibrate within you.

MEDITATIONS ON INTENTION AND WILLPOWER

The Buddha held the belief that as ideas go, the one that is developed and manifested is more important than the one that is not. Ideas, hopes, and dreams arrive like thistles on the wind and disappear just as quickly. That is, unless you capture and claim them. Using a laser focus that comes from a quiet meditative mind, you will be able to develop your inspired notions. Then with clarity, applying the right force of intention and willpower, and taking appropriate action, you will draw your ideas into physical reality.

RELINQUISH THE NEED TO CONTROL

In this guided meditation, you will discover how much easier life can be when you set an intention and let go of the need to control how and when it comes. You will learn to trust that what is not known to you will become clear and what you've called forth in intention will be manifested, not necessarily in your time but in accordance with the Divine Plan.

1. Keep your breathing natural.
2. Still the chatter in your mind by linking a numerical count to each inhalation and the words, "I am" to each exhalation, and repeat until you feel relaxed and your mind is quiet.
3. Mentally declare your intention—be brief and specific, stating your desire in a positive rather than a negative declaration. For example, avoid saying something like, "I don't want to hear bad news about my recent job interview." Instead, say, "I nailed my job interview and welcome the manager's call to tell me, 'You're hired!'"
4. Trust that the Universe has received your intention declaration and is responding in kind.
5. Embrace infinite possibilities as you let go and remember the old adage, "Each thing comes in its own perfect time."

VIRTUOUS WILL VERSUS WILLFULNESS

The Sanskrit word for energy—*virya*—(or vigor) is associated with exertion, endurance, and perseverance. In the Theravada tradition of Buddhism, virya is considered one of the five spiritual faculties (the other four are faith, mindfulness, concentration, and wisdom). All are necessary for spiritual work. This simple meditation on virya/vigor will guide you to an understanding of how this vigor or energy of the will must be taken as a whole, working in harmony with the other four virtues to avoid imbalance.

1. Sit cross-legged with your spine straight and your hands relaxed.
2. Close your eyes.
3. Turn your gaze inward toward a point at the center between the eyebrows.
4. Choose one of the five spiritual faculties as the subject of your meditation (perhaps the one you would like to energize or intensify): vigor, faith, mindfulness, concentration, or wisdom.
5. Contemplate why and how each of these virtues works best in a harmonious unity.

Imagine how the forceful expression of willpower could generate imbalance so that the five virtues are no longer balanced and working in unified harmony.

1. Consider how the virtue of concentration now must be strengthened to subdue the vigor of willpower and re-establish the harmony.

2. Grasp the notion that when vigor is excited into frenetic energy or willful force, calm concentration must be employed to restore balance.
3. Be mindful that when you wield your willpower in ways that align with a Higher Power, you ensure that your five spiritual faculties remain in a virtuous balance.

REDIRECT EMOTION USING INTENTION

Use this meditative exercise secretly when you've come away from a situation where you've felt overpowered with emotional energy. With anger, for example, verbally lashing out or getting physical doesn't subdue the anger; on the contrary, it can attract more anger from your adversary. Redirecting the anger to mindfulness of the breath can be a powerful tool for dealing with the emotion.

1. Sit in a comfortable position.
2. Relax your stomach, neck, and shoulders.
3. Close your eyes.
4. Feel the movement of your breath—cycling in, flowing out.
5. Mentally declare the following intention: I am letting go of anger and coming to rest in the cool, quiet peace of my soul.
6. Let your thoughts focus on the breath. If your thoughts rush back to the narrative about the cause of your anger, gently guide them back to feeling the breath and repeat your intention.
7. Shift the feeling of anger to the feeling of breath and soon you will realize your emotion is simply a communication tool.
8. Direct thoughts of loving-kindness toward yourself.
9. Feel unflustered, serene, and peaceful.

VIEW A VISUAL IMAGE OF WILLPOWER

This meditation focuses on the symbolic imagery found on the eighth card in the Major Arcana portion of a tarot deck, Strength. The image on this card shows a woman looking fearlessly into the mouth of a lion. Over her head is the symbol of infinity and at her back is a mountain. The colors red and yellow dominate this card. Place the card where you can see it while sitting for meditation. Contemplate the card's symbolism and how it relates to your power of will to take a stand, get things done, fight for a cause, change a habit, or succeed in some endeavor.

1. Sit with a straight spine.
2. Take two or three cleansing breaths.
3. Consider in turn each attribute represented by the card's imagery—self-control, patience, perseverance, endurance, fortitude, confidence, and courage.
4. Consider causes you believe in and do a self-check to assess what talents and skills you might have to help a chosen cause.
5. Decide if there is a particular area you'd like to work on in developing and strengthening your force of will for the greater good or to fight for a cause.
6. Devise a plan.

The Power of Will

Will is your ability to make a reasoned choice, control your actions, or decide to do something difficult.

A NEW HABIT BEGINS WITH INTENTION AND RESOLVE

Choose a healthy new habit like drinking a bottle of water first thing in the morning instead of reaching for a caffeinated beverage. Experts say it takes twenty-one days or longer to break a habit or form a new one. For spiritual seekers, it's worth noting that Eastern and Western wisdom teachers suggest aligning your personal willpower with that of the Divine and using faith and determination to stay the course.

1. Stand with your hands folded in prayer and set your intention.
2. Leave your palms slightly apart so the energy of the bad habit can flow away.
3. Lower your palms into open cups at your waist to receive the energies available in the Universe to help you establish the healthy habit.
4. Close your eyes. Adopt the Buddhist approach of resisting the temptation to think, feel, or do what is not beneficial and healthy.
5. Relax and summon your consciousness and dynamic will.
6. Mentally affirm your desire to align your willpower with the will and power of the Creator.
7. Focus your thoughts on letting go of the old habit. Release it.
8. Affirm your desire and intention to make the new habit a part of your daily regimen.
9. Be faithful in your resolve.
10. Reinforce your intention throughout the day with affirmations, reminder notes, and images associated with your new habit.

USE INTENTION TO MANIFEST SOMETHING DESIRED

The law of attraction is a philosophical idea that asserts that the power of your thought is always drawing to you positive and negative people, objects, situations, and circumstances. Mind chatter goes on endlessly, and since the force of attraction does not discriminate between good and bad thoughts, it makes sense to keep a positive state of mind. Formulate a clear intention and then infuse it with the belief that you deserve what you ask for; trust that what you ask for, you'll receive; and feelings of confidence, joy, expectancy, and gratitude. Use the following meditation technique to get started.

1. Sit with eyes closed.
2. Visualize a specific object you desire.
3. Mentally state your intention to draw your heart's desire into your life. Be bold and specific in your declaration. For example, if you want a string of beads to use for chanting prayers or a mantra, you might say the following: "I desire to manifest a *japa mala* of 108 sandalwood prayer beads from India tied with red string, and I am drawing it to me now."
4. Affirm you are deserving and ready to receive. Make a space in your life for the object.
5. Stoke a feeling of jubilation, feeling as you will when the object arrives, not questioning when or how it will come.
6. Know that a positive outcome is always possible when you yoke your willpower to the Unseen Power at work in the Universe.
7. Feel genuine gratitude for all that comes to you when you align your will with that of the Creator.

GROW A STRONGER BACKBONE THROUGH WILLPOWER

Have you ever put off telling someone your decision because you were waiting for the right moment to have "the talk"? Perhaps your talk is about taking a big step forward, shifting your career in a different direction or retiring, launching an entrepreneurial venture, or closing the door on a relationship. If you haven't found the right time, the right way, the right words, or feel like you need a stronger backbone to communicate the truth in your heart, try the following meditation.

1. Burn incense of sandalwood, the scent associated with your third chakra, the Manipura.
2. Sit in a comfortable position and fix your attention on this chakra's warrior energy to make a conscious choice to take action
3. Reflect on your power to choose whatever you want for your life and then make your decision about what you will do (ease of breath and a sense of feeling light indicates the right decision; nausea can indicate it's the wrong decision).
4. Imagine the warmth of the sun powering you up with the authority and will to speak your truth.
5. Notice how your senses of self-worth and confidence intensify.
6. State in a clear, declarative sentence what your intention is (for example, for "the talk" to be well-received and your decision accepted).
7. Visualize how well "the talk" will go as you communicate with grace, clarity, and confidence.
8. Feel a sense of release as you embrace infinite possibilities for a positive outcome.

USE INTENTION TO DISCOVER YOUR LIFE'S PURPOSE

You may feel perfectly in step with your life's plan and in tune with its purpose. But if not, use this twelve-step heart chakra meditation. Put forth an intention to gain direction if you desire to be guided toward your best life now.

1. Kneel on your yoga mat, sitting on your heels (knees together, heels touching).
2. Lean forward, allowing your forehead to come down to rest on the mat.
3. Place your hands, palms up, beside your feet. Relax your toes. (This is called the Child's Pose.)
4. Inhale slowly and breathe out through your nose.
5. Surrender all the tension in your shoulders and body into the earth as your thoughts follow the stream of breath in for five to ten cycles.
6. Rise back to the sitting position, making sure toes are relaxed, arms are at your back, and fingers are laced together before you stretch.
7. Keeping your spine straight and facing up, stretch backward to open your chest and heart chakra.
8. Inhale and feel blessings for knowledge and all you need in your life coming to you.
9. Exhale and feel the release of that which you don't need in your life floating away. Repeat the inhale/accept and exhale/release for five to ten cycles.

10. Move out of that pose to rest in a cross-legged asana, palms open on your thighs. Feel your heart energy enlivened; mentally state your desire to have your best life now—to know your purpose and whether to stay the course or shift in a new direction.
11. Rest in heart-centered awareness.
12. Note feelings of peace versus uneasiness (yes/no responses from your intuition).

ALIGN YOUR WILL WITH WORKS TO BENEFIT THE EARTH

American Tibetan Buddhist Pema Chödrön counsels that "meditation is about opening and relaxing to whatever arises." In meditation, you might receive inspiration to work in the world in ways you hadn't consciously anticipated. For example, maybe you've always been a nature lover and feel inspired to protect Mother Earth but don't know how to start or where to take your desire. Use those questions as you undertake a meditative nature walk. Let your intuitive thoughts and limitless mind bring forth ideas during your walk.

Put on your walking shoes and head out into nature—to the nearest park, into the woods, or across a field.

1. Walk as Thich Nhat Hanh suggests: ". . . as if you are kissing the earth with your feet."
2. Feel light in your body.
3. Notice the in and out of your breaths.
4. Focus your mind on ways to honor and engage in a peaceful coexistence with the planet through the use of mind and will; for example, you might:
   * Embrace nonviolence toward the earth
   * Recycle as much as possible
   * Restore forests/replant trees
   * Adhere to a "green" lifestyle
   * Preserve biodiversity
   * Revere the earth and all the life it supports
5. Write down new ideas with the intention to get them done.

LETTING GO OF HINDRANCES

It's easy to move forward when you don't feel restricted in any way, but for those times when you might feel held back or stuck, go into the temple of your heart and meditate. Mentally ask what is impeding your progress in yoga or on your spiritual path—it might be one or more of the five hindrances outlined in Buddhist tradition: desire, ill will, sloth, restlessness, and doubt. These interfere with meditation progress and daily life. For this meditation, start with a simple seated position and meditate on how best to apply your will to release one or more of the hindrances.

1. Sit on the floor with legs outstretched and slightly apart and hands placed at your sides on the floor.
2. Make your spine as straight and stretched out as far as possible (it might help to pull your buttocks apart slightly as you lean forward so you're seated firmly on your bottom bones).
3. Bend straight forward from your hips and stretch your fingers to your toes.
4. Deepen the stretch and relax. Hold the first hindrance in your mind—desire. Breathe in. Breathe out and stretch as you release desire.
5. Repeat the steps as you let go of ill will, sloth, restlessness, and doubt.
6. Lean back onto the floor and relax.
7. Rest in the infinity of your interior mental space and awareness that nothing can hold you back now.

MEDITATIONS
ON SYNCHRONICITY

An opportunity exists in each moment to notice what is showing up in your life. As you begin to make conscious choices about aligning your thoughts, words, and actions in positive and meaningful ways, you may notice, too, that your world seems to shift. Opportunities arise. Your circumstances change. New people enter your life. Coincidences occur. Your job is to notice, feel appreciative, and realize that you are connecting with the realm of all possibility. Imagine how you can design your future.

THE DOORWAY TO THE INFINITE

Synchronicity, a concept commonly defined as a meaningful coincidence and first coined by Carl Jung, is one of those universal laws affecting manifestation. Once you've put forth an intention to manifest something in your life, the law of synchronicity ensures that references to your intention begin to show up. The most powerful way to set forth an intention involves the space between thoughts. Ancient wisdom traditions have taught that this gap is the doorway to all things infinite—possibilities, correlation, imagination, intention, and creativity. Here's how to send your intention through that doorway and invite synchronicity into your life.

1. Sit erect with your palms relaxed and opened to receive.
2. Close your eyes and turn your attention inward.
3. Breathe naturally while feeling air flow gently in and out of your nostrils.
4. Notice how your stomach also moves with your breathing.
5. Take note of any tension in your body. Let it go.
6. Return to observing your feelings and thoughts, but don't judge—be aware.
7. When your thoughts wander, notice that, too.
8. Observe how each thought springs from another.
9. Notice the space between your thoughts.
10. Focus on that space. Put your attention there. Mentally insert your intention into that gap.

LOOK FOR LINKAGE IN MEANINGFUL COINCIDENCES

In Buddhist traditions, when two events are happening in a way that suggests cause and effect but, in fact, have no causal relationship, it's called interdependent co-arising. One thing did not give rise to the other, but there is linkage. Dr. Deepak Chopra has noted that a synchronous event happens as a result of an intention, whether it was conscious or not. It's important to pay attention to the synchronicity occurring in your life because doing so helps you see the interconnectedness of all things, helps you expand your consciousness from limited thinking, and presents a plethora of opportunities. Your purpose in life and its meaning become clear. The following practices are to be used in meditation or in your daily life to help you see linkages and recognize when synchronous events occur.

1. See yourself as a spirit connected to the eternal field of consciousness.
2. Form your intentions with clarity.
3. Avoid getting bogged down in the details of how you want something or someone to show up in your life; let go and let the Higher Authority deal with that.
4. Consider what is being mirrored back to you in all of your relationships.
5. Feel that your mind is in harmony and synchronicity with the mind of the Universe and, therefore, you can tap into infinite possibility and potential.
6. When synchronous events happen, meditate on whether or not there are karmic links and, if so, what might be their significance.

THE POWER OF INFINITE POSSIBILITY

Stories abound of ancient yogis who had the power to create or bestow health, wealth, happiness, and spiritual powers—even enlightenment. It is possible for you to claim that power as well when you set forth the intention to have success, abundance without limit, excellent health, dynamic willpower, and wisdom. Remember that you are the architect of your life, co-creating with the Divine Power that has created the Universe and everything that moves in it. Properly aligned with that Higher Power's dynamic force and wisdom, you tap into the realm of possibility and potentiality. You attract synchronicity into your life along with those blessings of health, wealth, happiness, and spiritual powers that you may seek.

1. Close your eyes.
2. Breathe in a natural, easy rhythm as you relax into a cocoon of peace.
3. Think of Divine Will as limitless energy (capable of creating solar systems or changing destiny, for example) guided by wisdom.
4. Feel your will attuning to Divine Will.
5. Know that the abundance from the storehouse of the Universe can flow freely to you when you unite your will with the Higher Power.
6. Before exerting your will, align it with that Higher Power so that you might tap into the highest source of confidence and abundance for success.

NOTE SYNCHRONOUS GUIDEPOSTS

"I am open to the guidance of synchronicity . . . ," noted the Dalai Lama. Synchronous events may be taken as auspicious signs that you are making progress in meditation. They are indicators that you are evolving along the path toward awakening to the spark within that connects you to the One in All. The Buddhist practice of *Vipassana* (insight meditation) invites you to be aware of and realize the inter-connectedness of all things.

1. Close your eyes and focus your attention at the third-eye center.
2. Count your breaths as you establish a deep, tranquil state for concentration.
3. Notice the chatter of the mind slowing.
4. Use the powers of awareness to "know" the mind, rather than "control" it.
5. Think about signs of synchronicity showing up in your life. For example:
    * Patterns of numbers, letters, or words repeating in your life
    * Unlikely but important encounters happening
    * The arrival of teachers/mentors/friends just when you need them
    * The ease with which positive situations and circumstances full of opportunities arrive
    * Messages or knowledge coming, just when needed

SYNCHRONICITY AND THE LAW OF UNITY

The spiritual law of unity asserts that we are all connected by a collective consciousness and by forces at work that we can't fully understand but may intuitively sense. The ancient yogis observed that nothing separates us. When you affirm the following before doing your yoga practice or meditation, you acknowledge the linkage (the power of unity) that exists between infinite consciousness and infinite abundance.

* My essence is pure consciousness.
* Pure consciousness is pure possibility.
* Pure potentiality and possibility encompass infinite creativity, out of which synchronous events arise.
* In my essential nature, I draw nearest to the field of infinite possibility.
* When synchronous events show up in my life, I will know the law of unity is at work, and I will look for the message in that moment.

Measure by Happiness

Paramahansa Yogananda advised his devotees to hold to a consciousness of abundance (attained through meditation) to experience mysterious forces coming to their aid. He further taught them to measure success by the yardstick of happiness and to remain confident in their spiritual endeavors.

THE ENERGY OF GRATITUDE

Mindful gratitude can generate more synchronicity in your life. Keep your awareness in the present. Notice and give thanks for simple blessings—the ability to breathe in and out without effort, to taste the sweetness of honey on your tongue, to smell a sprig of lavender, to feel the breeze against your skin, to hear the wind in the trees, and to see a shooting star. Notice these things in the moment. Feel in the core of your being a genuine appreciation. Give thanks.

1. Calm your mind and sit quietly.
2. Take stock of what you have in your life. For example:
   * An able, strong body
   * A healthy mind
   * Love of family and friends
3. Work through each bulleted item on this list (or one you create) by affirming each item: "I am blessed with a strong body."
4. Feel genuine appreciation for your body.
5. Affirm your gratitude: "For a strong body, I give thanks."
6. Go the next item and assert: "I am blessed with a healthy mind."
7. Continue as before in the same pattern until you've worked your way through all the items.

Challenges As Blessings

See all the challenges of life as blessings from which you gain insight, knowledge, mastery, and power. Seeing life's positives and negatives with equanimity as blessings and feeling appreciation for them opens you to the experience of Divine Grace.

DECLUTTER TO RECOGNIZE SYNCHRONOUS EVENTS

Clear your mental clutter (emotional baggage, psychological blockages, and self-defeating thoughts) if you desire to generate new thoughts, stimulate creative ideas, and spark spiritual connections. When your mind is less chaotic and more attuned to the Universe's spiritual laws, you'll notice synchronous events that yogis suggest are clues to your true destiny. To do this meditation, you will need a pen and paper and a safe and quiet place to do self-analysis.

1. Center your conscious mind to feel quiet and grounded.
2. Close your eyes and assess the chaos within.
3. Think of the distractions in your life and follow the next four steps.
    1. Ask, what can I release right now?
    2. Ask, what do I need to ponder further to find solutions and eliminate negative thinking?
    3. Ask, what can I fix through an apology or making amends and then release?
    4. Ask, what can I confront (with or without the support of a helpful, trained professional)?
4. Open your eyes and take the pen and paper in hand.
5. Jot down the answers to these four questions.
6. Close your eyes. Conceive a timeline (end date for ridding yourself of each item of mental baggage or clutter).
7. Consider a to-do list for items than can't be immediately released and need further action.

8. Open your eyes and write down your timeline and to-do list on your paper and put down the paper and pen.
9. Close your eyes and breathe deeply for three minutes.
10. Breathe out release. Breathe in peace.

MINE YOUR DREAMS FOR MEANINGFUL COINCIDENCES

"Sleep is the best meditation," observed the Dalai Lama. Sleep, while nourishing you and healing your body, can reveal similarities between the waking and dreaming mind. Culling your dreams can yield meaningful coincidences, moments of lucidity, instances of self-awareness, psychic predictions, and spiritual breakthroughs. Dreams are fleeting, so recall and meditate on them upon arising.

1. Rise from your bed and face east.
2. Inhale and exhale like a lion, making the audible sound of "ah."
3. Repeat two more cycles of the breath, inhaling and exhaling with the sound of "ah."
4. Slowly bend over and stretch to touch your toes; swing your hips from side to side to loosen your neck, shoulder, and back muscles. Feel the energy move in your spine.
5. Return to the upright position and stretch your arms, hands, and fingertips straight toward the sky. Swing your body from side to side to loosen your hips, shoulders, and neck. Feel the energy in your body.
6. Repeat the cycles of breath, making the audible exhaled sound of "ah."
7. Bring your palms together in the prayer position, with thumbs and fingertips touching.
8. Recall and record your dream on paper for later analysis.
9. Reflect on the transition stages between waking, sleeping, and dreaming. Let your awareness rest upon how similar life is to a dream, fantasy, and illusion.

THE UNIVERSE SPEAKS, YOU NOTICE

When you seek help, advice, solutions, and insight, you open yourself. Your psychic energy intensifies. This draws direction from the Universe in the form of synchronicity. Yoke your meditation to this powerful pranayama, let go, and trust in the wisdom of the Universe to send you signs and your intuition to rightly interpret the meaning.

1. Sit with a straight back, eyes closed, and the tip of your tongue behind your upper teeth where you will keep your tongue during inhalation and exhalation for the duration of the exercise (this is the Bee Breath pranayama).
2. Focus, and surrender your need to control to the Universe.
3. Inhale through the nose quietly to the count of four.
4. Hold the breath to the count of seven.
5. Open your mouth and exhale to the count of eight. Sound the "wha-a-a-a."
6. Do four complete cycles of this breathing pattern and then rest, breathing normally.
7. Mentally visualize a small black dot holding your fears, worries, and anxieties.
8. Push this dark circle from your solar plexus and see it disappear into infinity.
9. Draw in a golden light from your crown chakra (Sahasrara). Imagine this light as holding the wisdom of the Universe as you visualize the light moving like a stream of energy up through each chakra and out the top of your head, re-entering, and returning down.
10. Trust the guidance that this light brings.

FIND MEANING IN SYNCHRONOUS EVENTS

The Ajna or third-eye chakra (also called the psychic center of intuition, light, and cosmic knowledge) opens naturally in accordance with your own evolutionary process as you develop and grow in your meditative practice. The sound associated with the Ajna chakra is *AUM*, and when chanted aloud it produces a vibration believed to stimulate the important pineal gland located at the third-eye center's location in the physical body. An awakened Ajna chakra intensifies the sound and psychic intuition and bestows telepathy, clairvoyance, lucid dreaming, and expansive creative powers. The following meditation uses the Bee Breath (Brahmari) practice and the simple Child's Pose that places the forehead on the floor (both benefitting the Ajna chakra). Do not do the yoga pose if you have heart or eye problems, since this position lowers the head below the heart.

1. Sit in your favorite meditation pose with spine erect and eyes closed.
2. Direct your attention to the space between your brows.
3. Gaze at the third-eye center without straining and do up to ten rounds of the Bee Breath (for breathing technique, see the previous meditation).
4. Exhale as you move into Child's Pose (Balasana)—kneel on all fours and then sink back onto your heels and stretch your arms out forward. Let your head come to rest on the floor between your hands. Listen inwardly to the primal sound of *AUM* underpinning creation.
5. Relax.

MEDITATIONS
ON FRIENDSHIP

Relationships with others enrich our lives in so many ways, not the least of which is drawing out our innate talents and special gifts. Friends mirror to us our good qualities, block us from doing things that are bad for us, support us when we're down, and boost our self-esteem. Friendships nourish our spirits and perhaps nurture us like family. Feel blessed if your friendships are strong and enduring.

OPEN HEART, HAND OF FRIENDSHIP

Numerous scientific studies indicate that individuals with friends live longer than those without friends or a social network. There's nothing to lose and everything to gain by sharing ourselves with others. Many yogis and spiritual beings walk in the path of friendship through Divine Guidance. The following meditation follows a kneeling backward stretch known as the Camel Pose (Ustrasana) to open your heart.

1. Kneel on your knees and keep your hips and thighs perpendicular to the floor.
2. Place palms against the tops of your buttocks with fingers pointing downward.
3. Tilt your tailbone ever so slightly toward your pubis without thrusting forward.
4. Inhale and push your shoulders back.
5. Use the support of your tailbone and shoulder blades to arch backward, touching your hands to your feet in a single dropping-down motion.
6. Hold this pose for half a minute or as long as it feels comfortable.
7. Move your hands forward onto the front of your pelvis at the hip points.
8. Inhale and push against the hip points to lift your head and torso.
9. Lean forward into Child's Pose (kneel on all fours and then sink back onto your heels and stretch your arms out forward. Let your head come to rest on the floor between your hands).
10. Meditate on the Divine's friendship with you and how you could better express Divine qualities in your friendships with others.

CULTIVATE THE QUALITIES OF THE DIVINE

Paramahansa Yogananda wrote a beautiful prayer expressing a heartfelt plea to find the Divine in every thought and activity so that he might also find the Divine in all people. The greatest of all friendships, some might say, is the friendship you share with the Source of All Beings. It is the beauty of the Divine reflected back to you in the faces of those you love in your network of friends. If you would like to cultivate a closer relationship with others, do it first with your Truest Friend.

1. Enter the silence of deep meditation and then plunge even deeper, since the Divine draws nearer as your attunement deepens.
2. Meditate deeply on qualities associated with the Divine, including an empowering strength, inner peace, ever-new joy, truthfulness, and unconditional happiness.
3. Vow to work on developing those qualities in yourself as you continue on your path of meditative practice.
4. Mirror those qualities to others in friendship.

> "Teach this triple truth to all: A generous heart,
> kind speech, and a life of service and compassion
> are the things which renew humanity."
>
> —The Buddha

BE MINDFUL OF THE OTHER IN YOUR FRIENDSHIP

As with everything else in life, doing your best at building a meaningful relationship blesses you and your friend. When your friend is suffering, you listen with empathy, offer encouragement, and validate his or her emotions without judging them. In the same way, he or she reciprocates in your time of need. It's what friends do—transmit the energy of kindness to one another and take comfort in the shelter of their friendship. True friendship requires you to be fully present to your friend, mindful of self and other. The following walking meditation intensifies mindfulness.

1. Calm and center your mind as you set off on a walk to your friend's house or a favorite meeting place you two might share.
2. Walk with your thoughts anchored in the here and now.
3. Place your hands behind your back, right palm facing the sky and resting on top of your left palm with thumbs lightly touching (a variation of the Buddhist Dhyani Mudra, where the palms are in front of the body, the right hand symbolizing enlightenment and the left, the world of appearance).
4. Focus on the blessings of your friendship with the other person.
5. Feel gratitude for those blessings.
6. Hold your friend in your heart as you stay mindful in the moment.

BE A FRIEND TO THE EARTH

Our planet earth is both awe-inspiring and fragile. The Scottish American naturalist John Muir declared, "The clearest way into the Universe is through a forest wilderness." With some areas of forest under threat, it's perhaps more important than ever to be a friend to the earth. Nature speaks directly to the senses—drawing you outward and inward at the same time and fostering a deep, abiding sense that the earth (which some see as a living entity) is due our respect, gratitude, protection, and enduring friendship. Meditate on ways you might honor and befriend the earth.

1. Enter meditation in Nature, aligned with the natural world, and be fully aware and present to it.
2. Feel open, serene, and relaxed as your senses soak up the setting.
3. Let your awareness take in the sounds, scents, and sensations, but don't get caught up. Instead allow your senses to anchor you into being fully attentive and present.
4. Sense the interconnectedness between you and your setting.
5. Observe how sharp your senses become as you sit in mindful awareness.
6. Allow Nature to buoy and nourish your spirit as you sink into the rapture of inner quietude.
7. Feel at one with all in your natural setting.
8. Expand your consciousness to include Oneness with all of Nature and then the Universe.
9. Feel humbled, inspired, and grateful to your friend, the earth.

BE A COMPASSIONATE FRIEND TO ALL CREATURES

Perhaps you already know the joys of being an animal lover and have rescued, adopted, or purchased a pet. Working on behalf of animals to protect and improve their lives is an admirable endeavor; for some, it's a calling. And being a pet parent has health benefits, too. Studies have shown that interacting with animals generates the release of oxytocin, that feel-good love/hug hormone in humans. Petting a dog has been found to lower blood pressure in the human doing the petting. Heart-attack patients with pets live longer than those without pets. Here's what you can do to honor the first precept in Buddhism, which is not to kill people, animals, or insects.

1. Sit in a steady posture with a straight spine.
2. Close your eyes and focus on the third-eye center.
3. Breathe in and out several cleansing breaths to calm your thoughts.
4. Focus on natural, slow breathing.
5. Meditate on *ahimsa*, a word derived from the Sanskrit root *himsa*, meaning "do no injury, do no harm to any living creature."
6. Consider how veneration of all species of life gives rise to a compassionate heart and how a compassionate heart can give rise to the moral and ethical desire to help every living being reach spiritual enlightenment (the Buddhist nirvana).
7. Focus on the Divine Spark within you. Visualize that spark connecting you to all living beings. Send energy from your compassionate heart to them.

WHERE YOU SEE DARKNESS, SHINE A LIGHT

When faced with darkness, become a beacon of light. Be an exemplar of humility, civility, patience, compassion, kindness, sincerity, and—above all—calmness. Cultivate virtuous qualities so that they are always part of your being. Behaving with benevolence can turn a foe into a friend.

1. Sit with a straight spine. Close your eyes and tune in to your heart as you breathe naturally in a slow pattern.
2. Visualize a beautiful temple. See yourself crossing a peaceful lake that washes away all negativity as you prepare to enter the temple.
3. Let the temple light embrace you as the inner sound of tinkling bells rings out your presence.
4. Touch your palms together in the Namaste Mudra to greet the Divine Presence within.
5. Call forth an individual with whom you've had a negative encounter.
6. Welcome him or her into the temple's sacred space.
7. Feel the energy of the Divine in your heart chakra. Feel your whole body become energized as the scent of roses permeates the temple space, and observe the same light, scent, and energy surrounding the person you hold in your heart.
8. Observe how the darkness dissipates in the numinous presence of the Sacred.
9. Fix your thoughts on the Divine in all hearts.
10. Rest in the holy, healing light of friendship.

TREASURE SPIRITUAL FRIENDS

The Buddha emphasized the importance of having like-minded spiritual friends. Such friendships help you develop, evolve, and eventually reach liberation (enlightenment). But what if you don't have friends who share your spiritual thinking and values or follow your chosen path? Consider meditation for clarity and the power of positive thinking to attract into your orbit like-minded souls.

1. Quiet your mind.
2. Mentally consider the qualities you'd want in a friend.
3. Begin Alternate Nostril Breathing (Nadi Shodhana)—use your right hand's ring finger and pinkie to close the left nostril.
4. Exhale and then inhale through the right. Close the right nostril with your thumb.
5. Release the left nostril, and exhale through it.
6. Inhale through the left nostril. Close it with your ring finger and pinkie.
7. Releasing your thumb, exhale through the right nostril.
8. Inhale through the right nostril. Close it with your thumb; open the left nostril and exhale through it. This completes one round of breathing. Do three or four rounds.
9. Relax, breathing normally and slowly. Notice the space between each breath.
10. Form a succinct intention that you insert in that space.
11. Feel joyful and expectant that forces are already aligning to bring you that like-minded spiritual friend.
12. Broadcast your heartfelt gratitude to the ever-giving Universe.

HEART-CENTERED LOVE FOR MAN'S BEST FRIEND

A canine cop trusts the trained police dog at his side—his partner—with his life. Guide dogs provide life-saving functions for people with mobility impairments, loss of sight or hearing, and afflictions such as seizures, mental illness, and diabetes. In theaters of war, dogs protect soldiers by sniffing out dangerous weaponry and also provide psychiatric support for veterans. Send love and appreciation to these four-footed friends who serve through the bonds of friendship and devotion.

1. Sit up straight. Close your eyes and breathe naturally.
2. Exhale, visualizing an energy stream rising along the Pingala channel (right side of the spine) from your root chakra to your crown chakra (Sahasrara).
3. Inhale, visualizing the energy descending in the Ida channel on the left side from your crown to your tailbone (Muladhara chakra). This constitutes one cycle of looping your energy.
4. Do four cycles of looping the energy.
5. Visualize energy swelling in your heart as you hold the thought of service animals.
6. Inhale, drawing more light to the luminescent pink bubble of love.
7. Exhale and visualize pushing outward into the world that bubble of loving energy to service animals.
8. Affirm: "Through the power and grace of the Divine, I send gratitude to you and the many selfless beings who serve in friendship."

FIND FRIENDS IN OTHER CULTURES

Social networking sites help us to experience a wider world, but there's nothing like international travel to foster a sense of interconnectedness. Through travel, you find people share the same hopes and dreams—love of family, robust health, happy children, the means to meet their needs, and friends to enrich their lives. To draw friends from other cultures into your life, do the following:

* Be approachable, friendly, and generous with your smiles.
* Spread happiness wherever you go.
* Be inquisitive, interested, and truthful.
* Show respect and actively listen to conversations with others.
* Resist measuring people by your cultural yardstick.
* Be the friend to others that you would have them be to you.

1. Quietly sit in a chair with a back support or in an asana that allows you to feel totally relaxed.
2. Close your eyes and take a couple of deep breaths.
3. Focus on the throat center (Vishuddha chakra) and listen to the inner sound of *AUM* (cosmic vibration of the Universe) or deepen your focus by counting your breaths.
4. Dive into the space between breaths, affirming to the Universe: "I am now drawing into my life friends from other cultures in the world that interest me (add any specific countries or cultures)."
5. Notice the energy in your body coalescing around this intention; let joy and expectation build.
6. Feel confident and appreciative as you offer silent thanks.

BE FRIENDS TO THOSE LESS FORTUNATE

Consideration of others is a spiritual quality to be cultivated—one that saints and sages of all religions through time have valued as a moral imperative. Attune your intuition to what your Higher Self tells you regarding contact and friendship with those living on the fringes of society as you meditate on the sacral chakra (Svadhisthana), which is associated with your healthy relationships with others.

1. Sit on the floor holding your head in alignment with your spine and sitting bones.
2. Place a drop of orange, bergamot, ylang-ylang, or sandalwood essential oil on your palm and rub your hands together (the color orange and these oils are associated with the sacral chakra).
3. Start this meditation with five slow and even cycles of breath.
4. Put your mind's focus on your sacral chakra (Svadhisthana).
5. Rub your palms together several times to create energy and heat.
6. Place your palms over your pelvic area beneath your belly button.
7. Move into the wide-angle pose known as Upavistha Konasana by putting your feet straight out in front of you on the floor; open your legs to a ninety-degree angle and lean forward. Use your hands (placed in front of you on the floor) to lean forward and open your hips wider. Use a pillow under your hips, if necessary.
8. Feel the warmth as you affirm: "I am able to initiate and nurture healthy relationships with others of all stations in life."

MEDITATIONS ON LOVE AND COMPASSION

In Hinduism's pantheon of dieties, Kamadeva, god of love, is depicted holding a sugar bow and an arrow of flowers that suggest that love's qualities are sweet and sensual and sexual. These qualities are impediments to enlightenment in the Buddhist tradition. Hinduism and Buddhism have identified categories of love deemed more pure and noble such as devotional love for the Divine or a self-sacrificing love that places the highest welfare of other sentient beings over romantic love. The aim of sages from many great spiritual traditions has been to know God as love and to lose their sense of individual self in absorption of Divine Love.

BREATHING A CIRCLE OF LOVE

If you project a straight line into space, it eventually comes back as a circle. Love is like that, too. The adage, "What you send out comes back to you" is true. Send love to others and also open a channel to draw the flow of Divine Love into you and you will establish a never-ending circle. The following meditation focuses on love as characterized by the Buddhist bodhisattva (someone who has attained enlightenment but remains outside of nirvana—freedom from endless cycles of birth and death, karma, and suffering—until all others reach enlightenment).

1. Practice Alternate Nostril Breathing until you feel centered and grounded.
2. Close your eyes and breathe naturally.
3. Rest in heart-chakra awareness of a warm and loving appreciation of the Self.
4. Be present to how this feels, what this means. Do you need to forgive yourself or others to completely open your heart? Do you need to set a specific intention? If so, do that with an affirmation.
5. Draw your focus away from self-love into an expansion of consciousness that embraces love for all beings.
6. Breathe in and visualize a golden light filling your consciousness and spreading throughout your being.
7. Affirm: "I am a channel for Divine Love."
8. Exhale and visualize a radiant stream of unconditional love flowing outward in all directions from your heart.
9. Affirm: "My love is ever-expanding to include all beings."
10. Imagine unconditional love flowing in and out in an unbroken circle.

GIFTS OF THE RED LOTUS

In Indian tradition, Avalokiteshvara, whose name means "one who looks down (at the world or in compassion)," embodies the compassion of all Buddhas. This bodhisattva is pictured in a Tibetan Buddhist mandala holding a red lotus in his hand. An important symbol in Buddhist sacred art, the lotus emerges from the mud to open into a pristine flower of many petals. In resonance with the lotus flower symbolism, Buddhists believe that humans can rise above the muck of the world to become beautiful spiritual beings and Buddhas. See what gifts of love you discover when you meditate on the heart-centered qualities of love and compassion associated with this enlightened being and the red lotus.

1. Chant *AUM* to raise the vibration in the room.
2. Breathe quietly until your body and mind have settled into a rhythm of Oneness.
3. Enter your home—the hearth of your heart.
4. Look inward and listen deeply for the inner *AUM*.
5. Visualize the red lotus in your heart as you consider the compassionate heart of a bodhisattva.
6. Gaze inward at the lotus to see a small bright light that emanates, which is (according to Hindu tradition) your innermost essence or eternal soul.
7. Feel the purity and intensity of compassionate love arising as you gaze upon the light within the lotus in your heart.

THE PRAYER WHEEL MANTRA

There are many ways to generate the positivity of love within. When you enter meditation and recite a mantra—perhaps one given to you by a beloved teacher or one you've chosen for yourself—change comes over you. That's because the mantra sets up a vibration in you and your space. Each mantra is based on a *bija* or seed (single syllable) sound within it that unlocks certain powers depending on intention and intonation. For example, *Hrim* (pronounced "rheem") opens the lotus of the heart to dispel illusion and bestow Divine Truth. A mantra especially revered in Tibet but also treasured by Buddhists the world over is *Om Mani Padme Hum*. The Dalai Lama has translated these four words as "The jewel is in the lotus" or "Praise to the jewel in the lotus." So beloved is the mantra (and the energy it imparts) that it is commonly found on stones, prayer flags, wall-mounted prayer wheels, rugs, and jewelry in Tibet, India, and Nepal. See how this mantra generates a shift in your consciousness because of the transformative power of sound vibration during your meditation.

1. Meditate on the letters *A-U-M* (*OM*) as body, speech, and mind (these being exalted in the Buddha).
2. Focus on Mani, which means "jewel."
3. Consider Padme, which indicates "wisdom."
4. Reflect on Hum, which refers to indivisibility.
5. Contemplate the mantra's six syllables.
6. What does reflection on this mantra reveal to you through your intuitive higher guidance?

LOVING-KINDNESS
MEDITATION

According to Buddhist teachings, the qualities of love and compassion constitute the foundation for ethics, but it starts with loving-kindness toward the Self. Science suggests that compassion may have a profound, evolutionary purpose because we humans have mirror neurons that react to other people's emotions and trigger in us a desire to help. Radiating compassion without discrimination makes you stronger and more resilient and instills greater happiness. The following meditation guides you from loving-kindness toward yourself, to four other people, then to all beings.

1. Use a breathing technique to induce a calm, centered state of mind.
2. Offer a prayer such as, "I dedicate the virtues of myself for the benefit of all."
3. Think of four people to whom you will send love and then formulate an affirmation to help you arouse loving-kindness in your heart: "I am wanted and loved. I forgive myself and others. I feel my heart full of love. I hold in my heart the peace of the Divine. My loves call forth love, peace, and joy in all hearts."
4. Feel the loving-kindness toward yourself.
5. Visualize each of the four people. Think of them swaddled in love, peace, and happiness as you radiate those feelings to them.
6. Think of the four directions the wind blows and then radiate love in all directions to beings of all spheres and realms.

LOVE AND KNOT KNOWING

Knots found in sacred art are rich with meaning. Often they are plaited or interlaced in such a way as to reveal no loose ends—thus, giving them an endless interconnected appearance. The paths patterned in the Celtic mystic knot find resonance in the endless knot considered a sacred symbol in Buddhism. The former suggests the interconnectedness of all things and the endless cycle of existence; the latter symbolizes the union of wisdom and compassion. Check out online images of the aforementioned knots before doing this meditation, which includes Cobra Pose (easy) to open the chest and bring energy to the heart chakra.

1. Lie on your mat and gently stretch to warm and loosen all your muscles and joints.
2. Get the energy flowing around your heart chakra with Cobra Pose (Bhujangasana).
3. Lie flat on your stomach with your forehead and feet on the floor.
4. Keep your pelvis on the floor. Breathe in while using your back and arms to push your torso upward. Breathe out.
5. Keep your arms bent and push to deepen the stretch. Feel your chest opening and energy flowing into your heart chakra (Anahata).
6. Assume a sitting meditation position and calm your thoughts.
7. Visualize the knots' interconnected pathways, which lovers and spiritual seekers appreciate for the symbolism of the eternal. What special meaning does the knot impart to you?
8. Rest in a joyful awareness that the heart's love energy is your true essence.

SHOW YOURSELF A LITTLE TENDERNESS

Why do we find it difficult to be tender and compassionate toward ourselves? The next time you're feeling defeated, deflated, or self-critical, remind yourself that you are unique among all humans. Buddhist teachings assert that you must show loving-kindness to yourself before you show it to others. You'll soon realize that self-compassion triggers the release of those feel-good hormones that increase a sense of trust, empathy, contentment, security, and calmness.

1. Lie on the floor in a supine position. Feel appreciative for your body, intellect, and emotions, especially those that guide you away from danger and toward security and love.
2. Center your awareness on a person (or a pet) who cares about you. Allow this sense of being cared about grow inside you
3. Affirm: "I am powerful and capable. Loving myself, I am better able to love others. When I feel compassion for myself, I am more compassionate with others."
4. Concentrate on the Manipura chakra as you begin one or more yoga poses that open and balance this third chakra associated with your self-esteem and personal power. Try Downward Facing Dog (Adho Mukha Svanasana) for starters.
   * Move from the all-fours cat stretch (facing down) position.
   * Rise off the knees and lift your butt up and away from the floor.
   * Keep your feet and hands still on the floor so your body takes the shape of a mountain.
5. Return to a relaxed pose. Rest in self-kindness and appreciation.

AROMATHERAPY STIMULATES LOVE ENERGY

Aromatherapy is an ancient healing modality that uses fragrant oil extracted from plants to balance and enhance your physical and emotional well-being. Essential oil is used in Ayurveda and other holistic and integrative medicine practices for healing physical, psychological, and emotional imbalances. Reputedly, the rose possesses the highest spiritual and vibrational frequency of all the essential oils, so it's perfect for energizing and balancing the heart chakra as well as elevating your mood, imparting a sense of well-being, and inspiring you to share the love in your heart with others.

1. Place a few drops of rose essential oil on your heart chakra or in an atomizer near your meditation space (the scent stimulates your olfactory cells that connect directly to the brain).
2. Inhale through your nose. Feel peace descending upon you.
3. Exhale through your mouth. Feel your body growing lighter, as if the cares of the world are lifting.
4. In your third-eye center, visualize a rosebud beginning to open.
5. Watch this gradual unfolding of petals as your heart energy intensifies and grows.
6. Observe a numinous light at the rose's center.
7. Hold your gaze steady and watch this light expanding.
8. Affirm: "The Source of all love embraces me. I am blessed. My heart is balanced, healed, and nourished by the light of love."
9. Observe the light around the rose growing brighter, expanding ever wider.
10. Use thought energy to radiate the light of love into the world.

LOVE BY ANY OTHER NAME

The ancient Greeks had a thing or two to say about love, and one word wouldn't do. In fact, they had six words for love: *eros, philia, ludus, pragma, philautia,* and *agape. Eros* signified the passionate kind of love that takes possession of your senses, while *philia* symbolized the deep and loyal love between comrades who would lay down their lives for each other. *Ludus* was the kind of love exhibited by frisky young lovers, as opposed to *pragma,* the enduring bonds of love that empower couples to have a long married life. *Philautia,* or self-love, was viewed two ways by the Greeks: narcissism (not desirable) and self-love that increased your capacity for loving others. *Agape,* the highest form, was a selfless love for all people. This meditation reminds you to remove barriers to the flow of love—whatever name you call it.

1. Sit in your favorite asana. Calm your mind.
2. Reflect on how love perfects human relationships.
3. Consider how love holds you.
4. Think about how you love others.
5. Dissolve walls, boundaries, and limitations you may have erected to feel safe.
6. Let love flow easily without barriers.
7. Mentally affirm: "I am meant to love and be loved, to become whole and holy as love flows to and through me."

> "Wake at dawn with a winged heart and give thanks for another day of loving."
>
> —Kahlil Gibran, *The Prophet*

SEASON YOUR LIFE WITH LOVE FOR REAL SUCCESS

What's the use pursuing your career goals with unabridged passion if your love of work outweighs your love of your body and your mind is overloaded with work details? All arenas must be in balance. Additionally, you have to ensure your success in life. Use the following guided meditation to assess your passions in life and balance them with self-care needs to create real success.

1. Focus your mind on complete cycles of the Three-Part Breath (Durga Pranayama) by first sitting with your spine straight as you close your mouth and breathe in deeply through your nose.
2. Let your belly swell and your chest expand with each inhalation.
3. Exhale, allowing your belly and chest to relax. Breathe like this for a few rounds.
4. Begin to take longer exhalations and shorter inhalations in a slow and steady rhythm.
5. Do abdominal contractions at the end of each exhalation, emptying the breath.
6. Make each exhalation twice as long as each inhalation in a gentle, slow motion; do a few cycles.
7. Breathe normally. Fix your attention at the third-eye center (Ajna chakra).
8. Assess your loves in life—for example, work, hobbies, family, and self-care.
9. Determine how you may find a better balance in an act of self-love.
10. Set a timeline to change and follow through.

LOVE YOUR CAUSE

Do you have a favorite worthy cause? Perhaps you hold a strong belief that we need to empower women throughout the world, replant deforested acres of the rainforest, fund literacy programs, or protect animal rights. There are thousands of causes and myriad ways to help. People throughout America and the world volunteer every day for charitable causes they believe in. Volunteering your time with a charitable organization that supports a cause you care about is good for you, too. Giving of yourself to help others has some surprising health benefits—besides building self-confidence and purpose, volunteering connects you with other like-minded people and makes you happy. Most importantly, it counteracts the negative impact on the body of stress, anxiety, and anger. Consider putting in some time with a cause you love. Let this meditation help you get started.

1. Draw inward to find clarity.
2. Calm your breathing. Focus your thoughts on the pros and cons of volunteering. It should not infringe on your self-care or in any way create hardship for you. You want your heart chakra to be open with this work.
3. Zero in on what you love and feel passionate about—perhaps it's creating art with kids, teaching yoga to seniors, or building a community garden.
4. Figure out if you want to volunteer with a formal nonprofit organization or start your own.
5. Come up with a timeline and an action list. With an open heart, follow your passion.

MEDITATIONS
ON GRATITUDE

Studies focusing on the effect of people's feelings of gratitude on their happiness and mental health reveal that expressions of gratitude impart a sense of well-being and increase optimism. Feelings of gratitude naturally arise as you cultivate kindness to others and demonstrate a generosity of spirit. When you feel a deep appreciation for a favor, benefit, or blessing that comes to you and express gratitude, you radiate goodness back into the world. This shows that what blesses one truly blesses all.

RELIVE A WALK IN THE WOODS

Naturalist John Muir said, "In every walk with nature, one receives far more than he seeks." During a walk in a forest, you can't help but feel an unseen presence that restores and nourishes. The fresh air clears the cobwebs from your mind, your muscles feel alive, and your vitality increases. Science says it is possible to reclaim the benefits of that walk whenever you reimagine it and that a feeling of gratitude is an important element of the experience.

1. Sit or lie comfortably with your spine erect but relaxed.
2. Notice your cycles of breath.
3. Slowly move your awareness from the top of your head down through your torso, arms, and hands, releasing stored tension.
4. Move your consciousness through each part of your lower body, releasing tension in each area.
5. Now, visualize moving your feet as you begin your walk. With each step, notice the crunching sensation of woodland detritus on the earth beneath your shoes.
6. Breathe in the fresh air. Feel the sunshine and shadow on your body.
7. Relish the wind caressing your skin, clearing your head as you stroll on. Hear the birdsong, smell damp earth, and touch a large, sunbaked stone near a gurgling stream.
8. Sit for a spell. Soak up the tranquility before bringing your consciousness slowly to your feet.
9. Reverse the energy flow from your lower body to your head.
10. Feeling exalted and happy, express gratitude to Mother Nature for her gifts.

JOURNAL YOUR GRATITUDE

Dr. Andrew Weil, the father of integrative medicine, follows a simple regimen for his own good health—meditation, breath work, mindful eating, an anti-inflammatory diet, supplemental fish oil, plenty of sleep, time in nature, exercise, and—gratitude. Gratitude, like happiness (another ingredient for a balanced life and good health), comes from inside. There's strong evidence that people who keep a gratitude journal and write in it regularly have mood elevation that can last months. Having a powerful intention to be happier and more grateful is a key component. And writing a detailed analysis carries more benefits for you than a quick list. Get started with this simple exercise.

1. Grab a pen and some paper or a journal.
2. Sit comfortably and breathe deeply for four or five breaths.
3. Close your eyes and let your mind scan back over the past seven days.
4. Take note of any event that was unexpected or surprising and brought you joy or was positive in a way that triggered your appreciation. (Unexpected events and surprises impart stronger emotional impact. Thus, feelings of gratitude tend to be more intense.)
5. Open your eyes and record that event on paper. Write about how you see that event as a blessing or gift. Savor the warm feelings again as you write about them.
6. Create context and meaning as you integrate this event into your life on the page.
7. Close your eyes and feel thankful, but don't stop there. Keep thinking, listing, and thanking.

USE THE LANGUAGE OF GRATITUDE

If you have forgotten the language of gratitude, you'll never be on speaking terms with happiness, according to an old adage. As it turns out, expressing gratitude has measurable benefits—among them, increased happiness, less depression, and a heightened sense of well-being that is noticeable by others. Dr. Robert A. Emmons, a world-renowned scientific expert on gratitude, has said that grateful people develop a particular linguistic style that includes words such as *givers, gifts, blessings, blessed, fortune, fortunate*, and *abundance*. So it might be wise to not only count your blessings but also tell others about them in language that reflects their specialness. While you are at it, let your gratitude shine through sincere and appreciative language delivered with a gracious smile or a warm hug. The following meditation can help you develop an attitude of gratitude.

1. Do quiet breathing to still the mind.
2. Center your awareness in your heart.
3. Think of blessings you already have and feel grateful for them.
4. Start a mental conversation (interior prayer) with an imagined being, your Higher Self, or the Divine about three specific things with which you feel blessed.
5. Explain in detail why those three are special. Use words like those listed by Dr. Emmons.
6. Reflect on how you are loved and valued and your life has been enriched.
7. Feel contented and happy. End your prayer with an appreciative thank-you for all your blessings, especially those three.

MENTOR, LOVER, STRANGER, FRIEND

"Let us be grateful to people who make us happy; they are the charming gardeners who make our souls blossom," noted French novelist Marcel Proust.

Examine your life for the gardeners who helped you in some way to blossom. Expressing why you appreciate someone who has touched your life in profound and positive ways is an act of gratitude. Send out joy and appreciation and they will return to bless you.

1. Find a comfortable position in a chair or on a mat. Sit erect with eyes closed.
2. Take several deep, cleansing breaths.
3. Focus your concentration on the third-eye center.
4. Feel that you are at the hearth of your being in the home of your soul.
5. Mentally invite in the friends who are walking with you on this journey of life—people who've touched you in a special way.
6. Focus on each person, explaining his or her particular gift to you and why you view it as a blessing.
7. Elaborate on how the blessing affects your life today.
8. Visualize the next friend and repeat the process. Do this until you've addressed each, in turn.
9. Thank your friends; vow to write a note of appreciation to each during the week (and follow through on that promise).
10. Rest in the warm feelings of being valued by your special coterie of friends. As you go forth into your day, do good for others as your friends have done for you.

PRACTICE GRATITUDE

People who express gratitude are seemingly more alive, drawing joy, enthusiasm, and happiness from some secret energy center. They are more determined, focused, and optimistic about the future. More likely to lend a helping hand to others and show emotional support, they also enjoy stronger family bonds. They sleep well and suffer less from effects of stress and experience less depression. Use the following seven-chakra meditation to recognize the unseen gifts of your energy centers so that you may cultivate a deep appreciation for how they are expressing in your life.

1. Calm yourself while sitting with an erect spine.
2. Run energy from your tailbone to your crown chakra and back down as you visualize red-warm sun energy on the right side of the Sushumna and white-cool moon energy on the left.
3. Repeat this conscious direction of energy flow three times.
4. Direct your awareness to the root chakra, Muladhara—earth, tribe, family, survival.
5. Bring your attention to the second energy center, Svadhisthana—your sexuality, emotional connections to others, and your creativity.
6. Direct your awareness to the third chakra, Manipura—self-esteem, personal power, confidence, and courage.
7. Move your attention to your heart, Anahata—compassion, love for others.
8. Draw your attention to the throat chakra, Vishuddha—communication, ability to express your feelings.
9. Focus on the third-eye chakra, Ajna—wisdom and intuition.
10. Direct the energy now to your crown chakra, Sahasrara—interconnectedness to all and the One.

THE EARTH BLESSES YOU, YOU BLESS THE EARTH

The earth provides food, water, and air—the essentials for our lives. Turn your thoughts toward the earth and the ways the planet sustains all life upon it. Consider the silent power and presence of nature. As Celtic scholar, priest, and philosopher John O'Donohue noted, "Nature is always wrapped in seamless prayer."

1. Close your eyes. Inhale a deep breath and let it flow gently out of you.
2. Feel thankful for the earth and all the life it nourishes.
3. Inhale and exhale. For the water that bubbles up from deep, sweet springs or falls from the snowy mountain peaks, give thanks.
4. Now breathe in and connect your thoughts with the sky, the sun, and all the planets and stars that draw your thoughts into infinite space. Give thanks.
5. Inhale and exhale. Feel the air moving gently through your nostrils. Give thanks for the air that gives life and your ability to breathe it.
6. Breathe easy. Think about the cool, dark evenings of winter when the earth invites you to burrow down and connect with the taproot of your being, or the warm, light days of summer that call you outside to celebrate the light.
7. Let your thoughts hold ideas of how blessed you are to call this life-giving planet home. For the earth's gifts, give thanks.

HONOR YOUR DYNAMIC IMAGINATION

Increasingly, in a world that embraces a digital universe, cyberspace, and technology, imagination isn't just a trait employers want; it's almost an imperative. Creative imagination is the realm of the soul and has a force that is easily recognized. When you ignite your soul force behind your imagination to do your job, you soon realize how easy it is to cross the threshold between the work and your interiority—where everything is possible. As Albert Einstein famously pointed out, "Imagination is more important than knowledge." Gratitude is a gracious acknowledgement of all that comes your way to bless, encourage, support, and lighten your heart.

1. Sit in a comfortable meditation pose. Breathe gently.
2. Focus on your heart center and offer thanks to the Source of All for what you've already been given (knowledge, inspiration, education, literature, mentors, teachings) and all that you continue to receive that inspires and fuels your dynamic imagination.
3. Next, breathe in and focus on your parents, grandparents, and ancestors, whose genetic material has given rise to your beautiful mind and astonishing creativity.
4. Focus on your health and offer thanks for a resilient vehicle (your body) in which to travel the unpredictable road of life and also a temple for you to find your real Self.
5. Feel gratitude for your brain that is strong, knowledgeable, and receptive.
6. Tenderly thank the Universe for the gift of life itself.

GRATITUDE FOR VETERANS AND WOUNDED WARRIORS

For the love of this country, there are many in the various branches of the armed forces in America willing to make the ultimate sacrifice. Regardless of your feelings about conflict and war, know that these brothers and sisters are working hard every day upholding their promise to preserve and defend liberty with their lives. Far from home, some bear silent wounds that only the Divine can fathom. Others have come home with injuries that have changed the trajectory of their lives. Gracious prayers of gratitude can serve as a silent healing balm for those wounded souls and their families.

1. Banish restlessness and quiet your mind. Breathe the Alternate Nostril pranyama (Nadi Shodhana) until your mind is calm and centered.
2. Enter into the shelter of your heart, where wounding can be cradled and healed in the privacy of sacred darkness.
3. Hold in your mind's eye the image of someone who serves.
4. Ask for the Divine Light to shine forth brightly and wrap this soul in a blanket of healing energy so that he or she may be restored to perfect health.
5. Now radiate the light that fills your heart to all U.S. servicemen and women who are defending this nation. Gently offer your gracious and loving thanks.

A WORLD OF HUMANITARIAN WORK

The goal of a humanitarian is to save lives, first and foremost, but also to reduce suffering and preserve human dignity. Humanitarian activities are wide-ranging and depend on the dedication and hard work of aid workers responding to natural and human-made disasters. Perhaps you are one of them. If not, consider what single thing you could do to alleviate the suffering of another human being or to support an aid worker. From those of us who, perhaps, aren't called to do that work, such people deserve a gracious appreciation.

1. Close your eyes and start your meditation with an affirmation from your heart center: "Today I will remember the Creator's children the world over. Those who care for them are precious souls, deserving of support, love, and gratitude. For them all, I give thanks."
2. Focus on your heart and mentally affirm: "I send my soul's peace to those who are weary, weeping, hungry, or need a smile."
3. Deepen your gaze. Imagine a lotus with many petals with a small, bright light within.
4. Inhale deeply and as you exhale, see the petals fluttering and opening to expose this light that emanates love. Now feel love and gratitude rising in your heart.
5. Breathe in and exhale as the feelings expand.
6. Radiate this appreciation to the world's aid workers and the individuals they help.
7. Feel saturated in the gracious peace and light of the Divine.

GRATITUDE FOR COURAGE DURING UNSPEAKABLE LOSS

In Buddhism, giving is the greatest of virtues. People with failing organs, for instance, depend on organ donations to go on living. But for the families who are suffering the shock of a sudden loss, the decision to donate must come quickly, even as they are struggling with grief. To donate an organ is to give a priceless gift to a stranger. It's a heroic and virtuous act by compassionate souls. Although these individuals have no direct connection to the unfolding of your personal story, in a larger context, they do. Think of a unified field in which we are all points of pulsating light held in a continuum by a powerful force.

1. Focus on a single thing—a mantra, the smell of lit incense, the darkness behind the sheets of your eyelids, or the sound of *AUM*.
2. Visualize tension as darkness; breathe it out with each exhalation.
3. Visualize the light of the Divine as calm and restorative energy. Breathe it in.
4. Imagine peering through a lens revealing the magic in the ordinary—widen your view to perceive particles of light, tiny and almost imperceptible, colliding and bouncing off each other.
5. Observe this field becoming more expansive.
6. Consider each particle in this sacred, cosmic light dance as one living thing remaining separate and yet connected in an intimate reality of Oneness.
7. Let your heart perceive directly the experience of the Oneness in all. As gratitude flows through your being in the sound of *AUM*, in the light, and through the breath, give voice in your chant to the gratitude you feel for all these points of light.

MEDITATIONS ON FORGIVENESS AND MERCY

The Buddha taught the importance of purifying your heart to let go of sensual yearning and self-attachment and to also show compassion and loving-kindness toward self and others. At the heart of Christianity is a directive to forgive. In Judaism, forgiveness is associated with justice that requires an acknowledgement of wrongdoing, an apology, and a commitment to not repeat the error. Because everything in creation is evolving and changing in each moment, perhaps the easiest way to forgive is to realize that the wrongdoer is no longer the same person as the individual who committed the error.

DON'T SWEAT THE SMALL STUFF

Consider the possibility that the grumpy boss, fussy gym partner, or obstinate roomie with a false sense of entitlement just showed up in your life to test your mettle. That might be true, thanks to the mysterious workings of the Universe. The important thing is to see the interconnectedness of all things—not just people you like. It takes courage to work on empathy, forgiveness, and mercy to extend the hand of friendship to someone you see as an adversary or someone with imperfections. However, in so doing you may begin to glimpse a compassionate Universe.

1. Close your eyes and sit quietly with your spine straight.
2. Be aware and anchored in the moment.
3. Notice your breath and marvel at the mystery of breath—it gives life through Divine Grace.
4. Focus on someone with whom you experience conflict.
5. Inhale deeply and exhale.
6. Ask yourself: If this person were a mirror, what would he or she be reflecting back at me?
7. Take another deep breath; let it go.
8. Ask yourself: How does removing my ego change the relationship?
9. Breathe in and out, remembering that yoga is about detaching from *chitta vrittis*, or mind waves, to find equanimity, and view the relationship with perspective.
10. Breathe in and out. Direct the energy of appreciation telepathically as though it were a thread connecting your heart to the core of that other soul.

THE WAY TO FORGIVENESS

Blame and forgiveness have a yin-yang polarity that finds resonance in Taoist philosophy. Opposites such as life and death, good and evil, darkness and light, and positive and negative are two sides of the same coin. In Taoism, taking away one eliminates the other. Lao Tzu wrote in the *Tao Te Ching*, "Something and nothing produce each other." Not to forgive is to hold blame, harbor resentment, and feel bitter. Forgiveness is releasing the blame, opening your heart to growth and healing. When you realize that you are not the ego, but the Divine Self within—and that the Self can never be hurt—then you can clearly see there is no forgiving or blaming. All are one. In Sanskrit the word *hamsa* means swan, and the term aptly describes the gently, gliding pattern of breath for the next meditation. Hamsa is a natural breath mantra that is also known as the pranic energy or life-force mantra.

1. Inhale gently through the nose (making the sound "ham") and exhale (making the sound "sa").
2. Inhale "ham," breathing in light. Exhale "sa" and release any dark feelings you may be holding within.
3. Inhale "ham" and forgive someone you blame for something. Lengthen the exhale "sa" and release all blame.
4. Inhale "ham" and breathe in the Divine Power to heal and grow; focus on the exhale, "sa," and release any residual pain and suffering.
5. Continue the Hamsa breathing until you feel satisfied that darkness and light have been replaced with spaciousness and balance.
6. Rest in conscious awareness of the present.

SEEK SELF-MERCY IN THE LANDSCAPE OF BEING

Shock is soon replaced by anger when a sudden dramatic upheaval occurs in your life. You want to blame someone, something, or even the force of nature for your loss—the death of a loved one, the elimination of your job, or the loss of a pet or personal possessions to a natural disaster. Your rational mind wants to cry out that it's not right; someone's to blame. In truth, human malfeasance is almost never the reason why such events occur. But a soul's succor can come from a familiar landscape that renders solace. A flight into nature draws you gently back into the inner landscape of being. Draw upon your power of creative visualization for the next meditation.

1. Lie on your back in Corpse Pose (hands at your sides, palms open). Close your eyes.
2. Calm your heartbeat with quiet breathing.
3. Visualize yourself cradled by the earth or supported as you float on your back in a warm sea.
4. Feel the powerful energies of the earth or sea flowing into you. Breathe in.
5. Exhale what you don't want or need—sorrow, shock, anger, pain, fear.
6. Continue the visualization and gentle breathing until you are totally relaxed.
7. Enter the temple of your heart. Mentally affirm: "I am safe in the embrace of the Divine."

8. Relax into the awareness of simply being. Feel the succor of the mystical Presence, the one who knows your need for mercy before you ask for it.

Practice Being

Celtic scholar John O'Donohue said that in our desperation to learn how to be, our lives pass us by as we neglect the practice of being.

APOLOGY AND FORGIVENESS

In situations where miscommunication or a misunderstanding has escalated to an angry confrontation, the best way to deflate the hostile energy in the conflict is through an apology. Altercations can go quickly out of control—think of road rage, for example. Without someone offering an apology, emotions can produce a fire in the belly and knee-jerk reactions. Or if the emotions are stuffed, that can create further problems, since left untreated, wounds tend to fester. Consider these steps.

* Own the problem and apologize if you were partly or solely responsible.
* Forgive yourself. Show that you've moved on (especially if you must have an ongoing relationship with the other person) through kindness and gentle words.
* Do what you can to foster clearer communication. Be friendly.
* Treat the other person with respect.
* If the other person was responsible, cultivate an attitude of forgiveness, compassion, and empathy.

After the situation has been partly or wholly resolved, work on further damage repair in meditation. Practice self-love and compassion.

1. Sit in a comfortable asana with your hands on your thighs, palms up and open.
2. On the right hand, connect the tips of your index finger and thumb; keep the remaining fingers pointed out straight. Do the same on the left hand. (This is called Gyan Mudra. "Gyan" means "wisdom.")

3. Begin chanting *AUM* on each exhalation—sounding out each letter and holding the vibration as long as is comfortable.
4. Let loving-kindness and self-forgiveness enter with each inhale; release the emotions of the conflict as you exhale.

SHIFTING THE PARADIGM

Psychologists will tell you that when things aren't working in a relationship, it only takes one person to shift the paradigm. That means you can choose to admit defeat, keep the status quo, or change. You can't expect someone else to do the changing, to become the person you'd like him or her to be. You can only be responsible for one person's thoughts, actions, and behaviors—yours. You have to let go of expectations of change coming from the other direction. You are the architect of your life.

1. Sit in Lotus, Half Lotus, or a cross-legged asana. In both the Lotus and Half Lotus Poses, the spine is straight as you sit facing forward. Palms should be open and resting on your thighs. The thumb and forefingers on each hand form a circle. In the Lotus Pose, your right foot is pulled onto your left thigh; left foot rests on the right thigh. In the Half Lotus Pose, your right foot is positioned atop the left thigh near the crease of your hip while your left foot is tucked under the right thigh. Breathe slowly and calm yourself.

2. Clap your hands three times. Rub your palms together and feel the energy growing stronger.

3. Cross your palms over your heart. Breathe deeply.

4. Call upon your angels (messengers) or your Higher Self to guide you into inspired thinking about a particularly troubling situation.

5. Ask questions. Listen deeply for the answers that come to you through your intuition, which is your soul guidance.

6. Believe that the right action will become clear to you, as will insights into your mistakes and how to make a course correction.

MEDITATION FOR THOSE IN DISTRESS

There are at least four different meanings for mercy in English, but people the world over—regardless of the language they speak—understand mercy when they see it. Mercy in action demonstrates forbearance, pity, and compassion, and is a blessing. That is the mercy sought by people fleeing conflicts in the world and families without enough to eat or a warm place to sleep at night. Mercy compels people to action, motivating them to help strangers during natural catastrophes and man-made disasters. You can broadcast deep and compassionate feelings of mercy through prayer and meditation.

1. Sit with a straight spine and relaxed breathing.
2. Close your eyes and turn inward with your attention at the third-eye or Ajna chakra.
3. Keep your attention gently focused without straining as you mentally pray as a Buddhist that all beings might be free of pain and suffering and also free of the causes of pain and suffering.
4. Stay focused on looking inward as you breathe in and out slowly for twenty minutes, making the exhalations double the length of the inhalations.
5. Imagine people being cared for in places of conflict while breathing in and out.
6. Visualize families being given food, shelter, and warm clothing.
7. In your tranquil state of meditative absorption see people who are in all conditions of pain and suffering. For all of them and all beings who would benefit from kindness and mercy, radiate love from your heart to theirs.

TAP INTO YOUR INNER KUAN YIN

Kuan Yin, a bodhisattva in the East Asia tradition, is also called the Goddess of Mercy. Revered as an immortal in the Taoist tradition, she is much loved and honored in all Buddhist teachings. Her compassionate mind (*bodhicitta*) is to be emulated for the sake of all beings if you wish to be a loving, helpful soul in this life as you make your way toward enlightenment. Kuan Yin listens to the inner sounds of self-nature, or "the sound of no sound" in the Chinese tradition. She listens deeply for the cry of any sentient being calling out to her. It is said that she quickly responds.

1. Sit at a table and lean slightly forward with elbows on the table. Place your thumbs against your ears (to block the exterior sounds), resting your other fingers against your forehead.
2. Breathe in and then out. Visualize the white-draped Kuan Yin holding a water jar (symbol of pouring out compassion) and a willow branch (symbol of femininity and people of the world).
3. Listen to your breath sounds.
4. Plunge your awareness into the silence between the breaths and listen deeply for the inner sounds, possibly the high-pitched hum or buzz (the *AUM* of cosmic vibration). Absorption in this sound purifies the nadis and the currents of the mind and eases your path to enlightenment.
5. Mentally affirm: "I call upon the virtuous Kuan Yin to change my heart so I may always be merciful and compassionate when faced with others' emotional and physical pain."

NOWHERE TO HIDE

The Buddha taught that affirmations serve an important function on the path to enlightenment, and some sources say that the Blessed One used an affirmation just before he became enlightened, determined to stay focused on achieving his resolve even if his skin became sinew and his bones dried up. Affirmations reinforce your desire to stick to the goals and promises you've made. If you are suffering, do not attempt to escape, avoid, or hide from it, suggests Thich Nhat Hanh. Rather, put your mind right on it. Mindfulness can help you achieve clarity about the root of your pain and suffering. What you learn can foster within your heart mercy and compassion for the suffering of others and empower you to help them.

1. Sit in the cross-legged Lotus Pose (right foot over left thigh, left foot over right thigh).
2. Join hands in your lap—palms upward, with left hand cradling the right (Meditation Mudra of Buddha).
3. Close your eyes and fix your attention at the third-eye (Ajna) chakra. Breathe naturally in a slow, relaxed manner.
4. Focus your mindfulness on this inner world and notice what arises or calls out for your attention. Notice how your body responds to stimuli such as scent, sounds, taste, touch, and imagery even as the stimuli are being perceived as your eyes remained closed. The more adept you are at meditation, the likelier it is that you'll perceive the sensory triggers and responses, from gross to subtle and physical to psychical. What is the root or source of your suffering? Put your thoughts there and discover what it is teaching you.

WORKS OF MERCY, COMPASSION IN ACTION

Perhaps you've been at a hospital and seen the face of a courageous child waiting for a cure light up at the sight of a beloved sibling or parent. Or, maybe you've witnessed someone with a cheerful smile hiding the inevitable and approaching end to his or her life. Some people face suffering with dignity and grace, while others struggle with dreaded fear and a sense of desperation or impending doom. Aristotle observed, "Suffering becomes beautiful when anyone bears great calamities with cheerfulness, not through insensibility but through greatness of mind." When you feel ready to put your compassion into action, where will it lead you?

* Hospital
* Hospice
* Homeless shelter

* Courtroom to fight injustice
* Food bank to feed the poor
* Schoolroom

Or, maybe you'll join a humanitarian organization, treat people on a Mercy Ship, or—closer to home—do something good for someone who has done you injury. Meditate on that.

1. Choose loose, comfortable clothes and a quiet place to think, pray, affirm, and meditate.
2. Settle your thoughts, quiet your heart, breathe easy, and practice mindfulness.
3. Meditate on the question: What one thing could you do to ease suffering in the world, to put your compassion into action? Listen deeply.

MEDITATIONS ON SACRIFICE

Sacrifice has always been about the gift of life. When you sacrifice through service, devotion, and prayer, you are giving the gift of yourself (some aspect of your life) to another or to a transcendent reality. Sacrifice, whether for a person, community, country, or cause and regardless of the method and intention, strengthens your sacred bond with the Divine.

SACRIFICE FOR THE GREATER GOOD

The ultimate sacrifice of a leader is to release his or her power for the greater good of others. The South African anti-apartheid revolutionary Nelson Mandela exemplifies the sacrifice of a powerful leader. He spent twenty-seven years in prison (where he read, wrote, and reflected) and was eventually elected president of the fledgling democracy. Then, because he believed that the best chance of success for a post-apartheid South Africa was for him to transfer his authority after one term and step down, that's what he did. Not all acts of sacrifice have to be large in scope or done on a world stage. Any self-sacrifice to benefit others is worthwhile. When your heart and mind are of one voice, you'll know what to do.

1. Sit cross-legged in a comfortable position with your spine straight.
2. Rub your palms together and then place the heels of your hands over your eyes, fingers cupped over your forehead. Invoke the light of the Divine.
3. Move your palms together as in prayer (Namaskara Mudra), holding them at your heart center. Invoke the love of the Divine and give thanks for the Presence that is always available to you.
4. Place your hands in your lap, palms up, cupping the right hand with the left.
5. Observe the breath as you focus on the idea of sacrifice made with faith and no thought of self-benefit.

ALTRUISM, EMPATHY, AND SACRIFICE

On September 11, 2001, first responders raced into the Twin Towers. Many worked as first responders, but not all. Their efforts to save the people in the burning towers ensured that they, too, would be sacrificing their lives. In August 2010, in the Atacama region of northern Chile, a mine collapsed trapping thirty-three miners underground. By the next day, more than 130 people went to work to save the miners. A miner's wife gave birth during the ordeal, naming her newborn Esperanza (Spanish for "hope"). Countless people hope and pray even as countless others respond to emergencies through action. Both groups are motivated by a deep concern for the welfare of others. For some people, empathy drives their altruism. They feel others' suffering and choose to alleviate it, even if their actions could cost them their lives. Use the Child's Pose for this meditation.

1. Kneel on the floor or your yoga mat. Sit on your heels with your knees touching.
2. Keep your back straight and lean forward. Place your hands and forehead on the mat.
3. Tuck your head under slightly and slide your hands outward into a deep stretch, and then bring your hands back beside your feet, palms up. Relax your toes.
4. Notice how your energy connects with earth energy and then meditate on how service through empathy, altruism, sacrifice, and love is the raison d'être for all of us.

SACRIFICES CHANGE THE WORLD

When you give the money you were going to use to buy a new outfit to a hungry veteran, it's making a sacrifice. Or, when you offer a ride to a senior walking in the rain with groceries instead of attending that lecture you'd already paid for, it's making a sacrifice. They're small gestures, but if everyone made small gestures every day, imagine how much kinder the world would be. The Indian philosopher and pacifist Mahatma Gandhi understood, perhaps more than most, the meaning of sacrifice. He noted, "Real sacrifice lightens the mind of the doer and gives him a sense of peace and joy. The Buddha gave up the pleasures of life because they had become painful to him." Meditate on the value of simple sacrifices and how they can create spiritual threads that strengthen the bonds between you and others.

1. Take a walk.
2. Practice mindfulness.
3. Give the gift of a welcoming smile to each person you meet.
4. Notice how people respond to your smile.
5. If you see an opportunity to help someone, do so, even if it requires sacrifice.
6. Feel the lightness as the doer of a sacrifice.
7. Vow to do as much as you can for as many as you can and to relinquish the fruits of your labor by seeing the Divine as the real doer.

LIFE CHANGES REQUIRE SACRIFICES

Perhaps you are ready to make a life change in the arena of career advancement or a new job. It's more income, but the downside is the job takes you to a less desirable area of the country. You feel guilty because it means moving your family from a community they love. Does the move serve only you or will it be best for your family? Maybe the move is the right one . . . or not. Meditate on a strategy that will get you what you want without forcing you or your family to give up what's important to your core values and principles. Consider the following life areas included on a bagua, or feng shui map, before making radical changes, because a change to one area affects all the others.

* Health, family
* Love and marriage
* Wealth and prosperity
* Career

* Children, creativity
* Knowledge, self-improvement
* Fame and reputation

1. Breathe out the dark and breathe in the light.
2. Center your attention on the arena of life that requires a decision. Breathe in a natural, quiet rhythm and make a mental list of the benefits and sacrifices of making the change.
3. Ask your Higher Self for guidance as you ponder how making that change might affect your core values of love, generosity, compassion, integrity, forgiveness, and truth, for example.
4. Practice mindfulness until you are ready to rest and listen to what your intuition (soul guidance) suggests. Feel gratitude as you trust the answer will reveal itself if it hasn't already.

HOW TO KNOW WHEN YOU ARE SACRIFICING TOO MUCH

Followers of Buddha learn how to live a virtuous and balanced life through his experience and practice. Balance means that along with empathy, compassion, and sacrifice for others, you build into your life both time and energy for self-care and self-love. We've all known people who exhibit an immense generosity of spirit to the point that their self-sacrificing resembles martyrdom. It's an easy pitfall for those who are naturally self-sacrificing individuals. Seemingly, it's innately who they are. But it's important to re-establish balance before you realize you are living your life at the beckoning of others instead of for yourself. The following points are important to remember and worth meditating on.

1. Contemplate your sacrifices as a ratio of giving to taking. How much time and energy are you giving to others as opposed to what you are taking for yourself?
2. Ponder whether you feel you must give more than you receive. Reflect upon self-worth.
3. Think about how many hours of the day you devote to others and how many hours you take for yourself. Do you ask for what you need?
4. Reflect on how taking time and using energy for self-care will make you stronger, less stressed, happier, more loving, and more balanced. Decide to establish some boundaries so you'll have time to rejuvenate, such as through meditation, yoga, positive thinking, and living well.

THE CALL TO SACRIFICE IS A GIFT

Sacrifice is often triggered by a surprise or shocking event. A witness sees, hears, smells, or senses it. The person with a compassionate heart takes action. A man runs into a burning house to rescue a child. A woman plunges into the cold river to save her dog caught up in an undercurrent. A store clerk gathering shopping carts in a dark parking lot tackles a thief assaulting a shopper. In each example, the dramatic response happened because someone sensed the threat and took action. First responders face those types of sacrifices all the time—it's part of the job. Not so much for the rest of us. The point is that life will bring you surprises; they can show up at any time. Surprises are good—whether you answer the call to do something or not. They teach you about yourself (not the outward you, but the inner one). The German philosopher Friedrich Nietzsche advised, "Become who you are." Who you are comes shining through when you live life as your authentic self—from the inside out.

1. Hold your attention at the third-eye center and consider your best physical features.
2. Shift your focus away from the physical body and consider your best character traits.
3. Move your consciousness to your purest qualities and virtues.
4. Think beyond—peer into the heart of who you are at your essence.
5. Imagine your soul's reflection as a pinprick of light.
6. Visualize this light and countless others dancing with wild abandon in the ether.

SACRIFICE THE LIES OF YOUR EGO

You want to chuck your job. Every morning you have to play games in your mind to get up and go to work, but the voice in your head says you'll never again get another job like it. Or, you're doing lots of yoga to strengthen your core so that you can do that Scorpion Handstand with the deep bend of the back that's proven challenging, but the voice says you'll never be able to do it. Or, you jump through hoops to create a fabulous meal for your boyfriend's birthday and all the while the voice chides you, suggesting that everything you're making is so ordinary. Then your ego pushes you further and asks how you ever expect to lift yourself out of the realm of ordinary if you can't make a decent chocolate soufflé. You're ready to throw in the towel. Don't. Slather on the salve of self-respect and listen to your soul's guidance to sacrifice your ego for the company of the Omnipresent Spirit.

1. Take several deep breaths. Settle yourself.
2. Close your eyes.
3. Give thanks for the presence of the indwelling Spirit.
4. Reflect on soulful guidance coming into consciousness as you create space for it.
5. Mentally affirm: "I am attuning to Divine Will and listening for the inner guidance of Truth."
6. Feel the falling away of ego and body.
7. Rest in the awareness of light.

THE SHELTER OF COMMUNITY

With the discovery of fire, early humans rejected isolation in favor of coming together for food and companionship. Gradually, people created permanent shelters and formed communities. Today, people belong to groups in villages, small towns, neighborhoods, and cities. When you get to know others, you forge bonds. It's likely that you'd be willing to help and even make a small sacrifice if necessary to help someone in your community. Mahatma Gandhi said, "Gentleness, self-sacrifice, and generosity are the exclusive possession of no one race or religion." He and other Hindus stood with their Muslim counterparts, ready to sacrifice their lives for the stability of their communities during the violent and tumultuous period in India's history known as Partition. Contemplate sacrifice in your community. When you live in mindful awareness, you are neither looking to the future or constantly revisiting the past. Fully attentive to the present in each moment, you are in tune with your authentic Self, and your thoughts, words, and actions are in harmony. Thus, you exemplify to others the way to live with kindness toward all and harm toward none. Sacrifice and service brings goodness to the doer and the world.

1. Who is the memory holder for your community?
2. What binds people in your community together?
3. Who are the people who make your community special?
4. What sacrifices have people in your community made for the greater good of its citizens?

Use these questions to enter into a quiet meditation on how the Divine expresses itself through each individual and how that creates strong bonds of belonging in community with others.

THE CIRCLE OF SEASONAL SACRIFICES

The circle is an ancient and powerful symbol representing the eternal and what is seen and unseen. Gazing at the sun, moon, or earth, you see the circle. The earth's seasons are ever marching forward in a circular cycle. Just as autumn is chased away by winter's chill, the cold winter season likewise ends in spring's thaw. The gentle light of spring hardens into the glare and heat of summer. Then summer disappears as autumn arrives again. In the circle of nature, what has been born matures and dies, only to be regenerated. Throughout life, we see the seasons of the child, teen, adult, and elderly mirrored in the seasons of nature and human faces. You left behind the person you were to be who you are now. Sacrificing the old for the new renders the transformation in a steady, continuous flow ever moving between the visible and invisible realms.

1. Sit in a comfortable pose with eyes closed and bring your awareness within to your third eye of wisdom.
2. Use a pattern of deep, slow breathing to center yourself.
3. Reflect on what you love about this season or stage of your life and what you sacrificed to reach this point.
4. Let feelings of confidence, self-love, and appreciation fill you as you realize your life is exquisitely and uniquely yours—reflected in your gifts, talents, qualities, and traits.
5. Bask in an appreciation of the light and beauty of your eternal Soul.

MEDITATIONS ON HUMILITY

Humility is the opposite of narcissism and self-aggrandizement. Surrendering the ego is an important part of a spiritual discipline. In acts of humility, such as prayerful prostration before meditation, the yogi, yogini, or sadhak pays homage to the Divine and reaps the blessing of peaceful grounding.

CULTIVATING HUMILITY

In ancient Greek society, a person's talents, gifts, struggles, and weaknesses were duly noted and measured against the degree of humility he or she possessed. Humility was one of seven virtues stressed during the medieval and Renaissance periods. However, in today's world, we tend to notice humility in high relief against the backdrop of selfies and self-aggrandizement. When praise is heaped on an individual who has attained a towering achievement in life, and he or she responds with the grace of straightforward and sincere thanks, that's what humility looks like. Humility comes from the core of your being as a natural expression of your true inner character.

1. Lie on your stomach, forehead touching the floor, arms extended before you. Fold your hands into the prayer gesture (so you lie in the reverential prostration position of a devotee).
2. Inhale deeply and exhale a long breath out, and then breathe gently and deeply.
3. Reflect on the glory of all creation.
4. Settle into a gentle, mindful state.
5. Breathe naturally and attune your inner consciousness with the Source of All.
6. Mentally affirm: "Sacred Friend, come. Let me take refuge in your holy vibration. Help me to banish false pride. I am humbled when you shelter me in the light of your numinous presence."

> "We come nearest to the great when
> we are great in humility."
>
> —Rabindranath Tagore, noted Indian poet, playwright,
> and recipient of the Nobel Prize in Literature

THE SYMBOLIC COLOR OF HUMILITY

Take a trip to India and you will see Hindu priests in temples and yogis in ashrams wearing white or ochre-colored dhotis or lungis, traditional garments worn by men. In Southeast Asian countries, Theravada Buddhist monks wear robes of a saffron (yellow) color. The simple garb and colors associated with the sacred symbolize the renunciation of the material world by the yogis and monks. The wearing of the robe (a requirement for monks) sets them apart from materialist society and represents the virtue of humility. Yellow is associated with radiance, inner harmony, and vitality; white connotes sacred ritual, purity, reverence, and humility. Consider how these colors make you feel when you put them into your environment or wear them in clothing or gemstones.

1. Assume a comfortable cross-legged position on your yoga mat or sit in a straight-back chair with your feet on the floor. Place your hands in your lap, left hand cradling the right, palms up, thumb tips touching to make a circle.
2. Notice the sensation of air flowing in and out of your nostrils without controlling your breathing.
3. Focus your attention at the third-eye (Ajna) chakra and gaze upon (or visualize) the effulgent white light.
4. Deepen your awareness of that center of energy while considering the symbolism of white (associated with humility and also emptiness).
5. Meditate on merging your individual consciousness with the effulgent white light of cosmic consciousness.

HUMILITY ON THE JOB

The Dutch philosopher Baruch Spinoza said, "Pride is pleasure arising from man's thinking too highly of himself." A worker with a gentle spirit demonstrates supreme confidence and shows humility in the workplace because of the type of character he or she has developed. The emotions are balanced with clear and rational thinking. Consider, however, the worker who is overconfident and believes he or she knows more than everyone else and is brazenly arrogant. Do your work as if it is the most important task you'll ever do, Indian yogis suggest. In the ancient Hindu scripture *The Bhagavad-Gita*, Lord Krishna advises his disciple Arjuna to work to the best of his ability and to give up any attachment to the results, remaining "calm in both success and failure." The gentle virtue of humility is at the heart of the karma yoga the master is teaching his disciple.

1. Take time to sit quietly and reflect on how to balance pride with humility in your line of work. Vow to receive praise when you deserve it with graceful thanks. Don't say, "It was nothing," because that is dishonest. Eschew fishing for compliments.
2. Enter a quiet, single-minded concentration on why holding to a calm serenity is paramount.
3. Seek Divine Help on the job as you work to remain balanced even in the flurry of activity—regardless of how hectic and crazy work becomes.

SIGNS OF HUMILITY

Humility, according to psychologists and hiring managers alike, could be the key to success in your life and work. The following signs reflect modesty and humility.

* You look out for the interests of others instead of enriching your own status, position, and recognition.
* You acknowledge error, make an apology, and fix the problem by coming at it from another direction.
* You do not self-aggrandize or seek ego gratification.
* You're a patient and perennial optimist.
* You possess solid, enduring relationships.

Think of individuals you admire and acknowledge their positive qualities and virtues. Emulate them, and when meditating, approach the interior process of meditation and prayer with humility.

1. Read prayers or affirmations that show humility, such as the Magnificat prayer of Mary, Mother of Jesus, in which she proclaims the greatness of God and declares that God has "lifted up the lowly." Find the entire prayer in Luke 1:46–55.
2. If prayer is part of your spiritual path, use it to open and close your meditation. Spend time in interior prayer (prayer done with mindfulness of the Holy Presence can lead to the highest mystical encounter, according to the Catholic saint Teresa of Avila).
3. Enter into a silent meditation with your attention on your heart center (Anahata chakra).
4. Steady your mind and bring it to a one-pointed focus.
5. Invite the Divine to grant you the grace of true humility.

THE MEDIEVAL VIEW OF HUMILITY

In bygone eras such as the medieval period, the Church dominated people's lives. Consequently they were intensely interested in the subject of virtue and vice. They organized charts listing vices and the virtues that cured or remedied the vices. Humility topped the list of virtues, and pride was seen as humility's opposite. Abstinence, according to the list, remedies gluttony. Chastity cures lust. During that time people believed the number seven was sacred, so their lists included seven vices and seven virtues. It might seem a bit archaic today to keep such a chart, but introspection to root out bad thinking, bad activities, and bad habits is a good idea. This important inner work restores harmony and balance and builds character.

1. Reflect on what, if anything, you'd change about your natural way of being to foster not only humility but also virtues that benefit your character and your work on the spiritual path.
2. Think of someone you know who recently got praise or a promotion for a job well done.
3. Mentally see yourself showering that individual with recognition for his or her achievement.
4. Imagine others whom you might also duly acknowledge.
5. Hold them in your heart in meditation and invoke a blessing of grace for all.

GIVE COMPETITORS THEIR DUE

Success tends to puff us up; it makes us full of ourselves. It's human nature. When you work hard and achieve a major accomplishment, it is likely that you will be recognized for putting your heart and soul into reaching your goal. When it happens to a competitor, tap into your generosity of spirit and show humility. Honor the person's hard work to beat out the other competitors and celebrate his or her joy. Giving another his or her due takes nothing from you; indeed, it strengthens your character and engenders a sense of dignity. As the adage goes, what blesses one, blesses all.

1. While sitting, stretch your arms and hands (open palms) to the sky. Imagine a clock face and position your arms at ten and two. Fold your fingers into your palms and turn your thumbs straight up to the sky.
2. Open your mouth slightly and pant rapidly, but not forcefully, until tired. (Don't hyperventilate; it can make you dizzy and tingly.) Drop hands to your sides and rest. This technique brings more oxygen in and dispels carbon dioxide from your lungs while forcing belly breathing, to energize the body.
3. Sit with your spine and head aligned. See the energy in your body coalescing into a bubble of light. Send this light out to all your competitors. In this silent, generous act, notice the happiness you feel.

WHAT FOOT WASHING TEACHES

The practice of foot washing is an ancient custom of hospitality that predates Christianity. But through the Judeo-Christian tradition, foot washing has taken on a far greater meaning. For example, while it is common for a reigning pope to wash the feet of priests during a Mass of the Last Supper, Pope Francis broke with tradition when he visited a juvenile detention center in Rome in 2013. There, he washed the feet of a dozen prisoners, including two women and two Muslims. Some would call it a radical act—the supreme head of the Catholic Church washing the feet of women and non-Christians—but over the years Pope Francis has washed the feet of recovering drug addicts, pregnant women, and patients with AIDS. Through cleansing and blessing, his simple act demonstrates that it is worthwhile to humble the Self in service to the "other" and those marginalized by society.

1. Close your eyes and enter the vast interiority of the Self.
2. Call upon your inner guidance.
3. Focus on one act of humility that you could do once a year (say, before Easter or some other date of significance for you).
4. Reflect upon how, for someone on a spiritual path, humility before God (who is in all of Creation) is the highest virtue.
5. Listen deeply for the inspiration that comes.

THE HUMBLE PRANAMA

In modern India—as in ancient times—the gesture of touching some-one's feet upon arrival or departure is considered respectful and rev-erential and is also an act of humility. The gesture is not reserved for leaders in high office or revered spiritual beings but can be used with parents, grandparents, spiritual teachers (gurus), or anyone to whom you'd want to show respect. In turn, they may gently touch you on your head to impart their wish for you to have a long life of good for-tune and prosperity. So in this simple act of humility, a flow of respect and blessing happens. There are several versions of the pranama—in Sanskrit *anama* means "to bend or stretch"; *pra* means "forward."

* Bring the hands together in a prayer position and touch your forehead with your fingers pointed up (Namaskara Mudra, the most common gesture).
* Move your prayerful hands to your heart center and bend for-ward (*abhinandana*).
* Stretch out in a prostrate position. If paying homage to a form of the Divine represented by a sacred image or icon, point your hands toward it.

1. Start your meditation in the temple of your heart with a mental pranama to the Divine within.
2. Spend time in mindfulness to calm and center yourself.
3. Reflect on ways you ordinarily show humility and respect and what it does for you (the giver) and the other person (the receiver). It is important to do this because the "doing" might have become so ordinary and routine that you've lost the magic of the flow between the offering and the blessing.

PRAISE ALL THE GOOD THAT YOU FIND

Psychologists advise you to praise the behavior you want repeated and ignore what you don't like. That's helpful whether it's in a romantic relationship, in a work situation, or with family and relatives. Perhaps when you were growing up, someone advised you not to say anything at all about someone if you couldn't find something nice to say. At the heart of the advice is the reminder to be respectful toward others. Alex Haley, the author of *Roots*, was fond of the slogan, "Find the good and praise it." In fact, he had it printed on all of his stationery. The slogan became a precept for his life and one that he often shared with others. A powerful slogan written on a piece of paper that you often read or say aloud can be used as an affirmation for transformation. The slogan Haley liked has at its heart the virtue of humility. If you were to create one for yourself that emphasized humility, what would it be?

1. Take a walk. Practice mindfulness with every step.
2. Look around at humans busily involved in their lives.
3. Ponder the strength of a gentle message that conquers the darkness of disrespect.
4. Repeat your slogan often so that you don't forget it on the return home.
5. Make your slogan a part of your daily life, including the most ordinary and simplest of activities.

MEDITATIONS
ON HOPE

When you lose hope, life may seem pointless. This is especially true in times of massive change—whether in your personal life or in the life of the world. We all need to be light bearers of hope for ourselves and others. Hope inspires you to action to bring about positive benefit to your family, your community, and future generations who will inhabit this world. Meditation can help you find hope and bring about clarity in your thinking.

FINDING HOPE IN A NEW DAY

Start your day with the energy and light from the sun. In India, obeisance to the sun (dispeller of darkness and bringer of self-illumination) begins just before sunrise. Devotees greet the sun with a mudra and chant to thank the fiery solar manifestation for its gifts that sustain and nourish all life. When you start your day with the Salutation to the Sun (Surya Namaskara), its rays of infinite warmth, light, and happiness fill you with hope and possibility. The full salutation consists of a series of yoga postures, each with an accompanying mantra. What follows is one commonly used as the first position.

1. Rise to face the dawn. Wear loose clothing. Stand with feet together.
2. Join your hands in prayer at your heart, the pose of respect (Pranamasana).
3. Chant the first mantra: "Om Mitraya Namaha."
4. Continue with yoga poses that generate heat while strengthening your core or choose to rest for ten minutes before doing a sitting meditation.
5. Close your eyes. Imagine warmth and light permeating your being.
6. Imagine sunlight revitalizing all your cells, restoring them to perfection as the light becomes expansive, spreading throughout your body.
7. Feel saturated with happiness and confident that what you hope to accomplish will be easier having started your day with the sun.

THE SOOTHING BALM OF HOPE

Even when you do everything right, sometimes life throws you a curve ball that you didn't see coming. Taken by surprise, you feel knocked off balance. Your work is to aim for equanimity when such situations occur. Hope brings the light when the clouds of disappointment or despair hide your clarity and truth. "Hope," observed Thich Nhat Hanh, "is important because it can make the present moment less difficult to bear. If we believe that tomorrow will be better, we can bear a hardship today." Sit with hope for a while in meditation, asking for direction out of the hardship. Be optimistic that just as darkness comes, light also will come, dispelling the darkness. Opposites have a mystery of continuity—darkness shows up and then slides away when the light of understanding dawns. Hope can be the balm soothing your pain.

1. Assume a comfortable position and feel your breath move in and out through your nostrils.
2. Imagine the energy from your tailbone rising to the crown of your head via your Pingala nadi (feel the warm flow along the right side of the spine) and back down your Ida nadi (feel the cooling flow on the left side).
3. Bring your attention to your Ajna chakra, focusing on the spot between your eyes, and imagine an effulgent light (your Soul's light).
4. Merge your consciousness with that light. Attune your will to the will of God. In the Divine Power is the wisdom to solve your problems. Seek there the insights and direction for which you hope.

THE INNER WELLSPRING OF HOPE HEALS

Hope is a wellspring you find deep within yourself—in the end, it is you alone who either embraces hope or rejects it. In the India of long ago, people believed that if a holy man placed his hand on you when you were ill, you would recover. There is a similar process at work in the placebo effect, when a doctor gives you an inactive substance, instead of the real medicine needed to treat your illness, but you get well anyway. There is a powerful mind-body connection at work in both examples. The following meditation guides you toward seeing perfection in the cells of your body, because illness can't get a foothold in a consciousness of perfect health. But this is no situation for wishful thinking. You must be clearly focused and willing to take action to provide whatever the body requires.

1. Lie on your back. Calm your thoughts. Feel peaceful.
2. Put your mind at the third-eye center.
3. Make a clear affirmation for healing: "Healing is going on throughout this body, restoring it to perfect health."
4. Trust the process and feel confident that the complete healing you hope for will come about.
5. Practice mindfulness so you are alert to information the body communicates back through its chemical messengers to the mind.
6. Recharge your body with *prana* (life-force energy) through the instruments of pranayama and meditation.
7. Imagine the Divine Presence as the infinite Healer working to restore your health.

HOPE FOR CHANGE

Have you ever felt as if you've lost your mind? If you are like most people, you long for serenity when thought disturbances distract and impede your usual calm and clarity. This increased mind chatter can happen when you are multitasking or feeling emotional and unduly stressed. When mind chatter disturbs your thoughts, you miss the full content of each moment. But your insights into what's causing the excessive mind waves can point you toward change. You aren't bound by karmic fate to suffer through this sort of ongoing mindlessness. Buddhists claim that your awareness will provide insight and, even better, your insight provides hope for change.

1. Meditate in the stillness of a quiet space where you won't be disturbed. Sit in any pose that feels comfortable. Don't strain to hold a pose, since that will just add more mind chatter.
2. Pull your attention inward and close your eyes.
3. Allow free association of your thoughts. Let them go until they slowly decrease in their arising and falling away.
4. Mentally affirm: "I am the watcher of the mind. I feel calm and focused. I will ride the waves of my thoughts until they disappear into the ocean of peace."
5. Reflect on the change that is always possible through a shift in priorities, attitude, and action.

HOPE FOR A STABLE AND PEACEFUL WORLD

"Hope is the pillar that holds up the world," observed Pliny, scholar and the nephew of Roman scholar Pliny the Elder. Though Pliny was born in C.E. 23, he could have been addressing the modern world. Perhaps you, like so many others, yearn for a peaceful world—for not only the current generation but all generations to come. In August 1987, people around the globe hoping for world peace came together with a shared passion. They created the first global meditation event, known as the Harmonic Convergence. Groups gathered on mountains and other places believed to be energy centers to usher in the New Age of peace. The best of humankind lies in the hearts and minds of people who hope for stability and peace—not for just one group but for all. Moreover, as the Buddha taught, it takes only one person to shift a paradigm and to kill the will to kill.

1. Be at peace as you enter your meditation.
2. Release any inner conflict.
3. Let peace settle in upon your thoughts; let peace fill your being.
4. Imagine a golden bubble arising in your heart and growing like a helium balloon.
5. Radiate this golden sphere of peace from your heart out into the world.
6. Visualize the planet and conflicts everywhere ending as human compassion rises and flows in this golden atmospheric river encircling the globe.

A POWERFUL ELIXIR FOR RENEWAL

The earth renews herself in the season of spring after her deep repose in the darkness of winter. Only when she is ready does she awaken and drape herself in the splendor of spring. Many people use the first month of the new year as a time to renew themselves with self-improvement goals, hoping they can keep the promises they make. You don't have to wait for a new year to renew. Buddha revealed that you are what you think and whatever you think arises in your life. Your thoughts create your world. Hope is a powerful elixir for your mind and body. On a practical level, you can begin to release unwanted elements in your life to welcome in what you want, and as a spiritual seeker you can work on awareness of your True Self.

1. Take a pad and pen and sit somewhere quiet.
2. Close your eyes and center your awareness on what your senses perceive.
3. Think about the significant change(s) you want to make.
4. Break any big changes into smaller increments.
5. Prioritize the incremental changes, beginning with the one that will start you down the path toward the renewed being you hope to become.
6. Contemplate a doable timeline for starting your change.
7. Let go of everything that might impede your start.
8. Open your eyes and write down your plan.
9. Hold firm to your vision of the renewed you. Trust the process and let go of doubt.

CONFIDENT EXPECTATION IN CRISIS

In Judaism, hope is associated with the six-pointed star, the menorah and oil that keeps the lamp burning, and the goblet that holds the wine for blessing. For Christians, hope is kindled in the heart at the sign of the cross. Also, the anchor was an early Christian symbol of hope for those suffering persecution by the Romans The anchor suggested finding safe harbor. In Eastern traditions, the lotus stands as a symbol of hope for rising from murky depths to enlightenment. Regardless of how hope is symbolized in various cultures, it means basically the same thing: a confident expectation of a particular desired outcome. If you are battling an illness, a tough period in college, or a rough patch in your marriage, have hope. Science shows that people heal more quickly when they hold on to hope for recovery. Holding out hope, you trigger new thinking and motivation for working things out. You have a heightened sense of optimism.

1. Choose a talisman (a gemstone, a key, a wedding ring, a locket, a cross, or prayer beads, for example) and hold it during your meditation, drawing symbolism from it and infusing it with your energy.
2. Sit on the floor or a mat in a comfortable pose. Close your eyes.
3. Focus on your heart—go into the temple and dive deeply into the peace you find there.
4. Chant the word *AUM/OM* or *shanti* (peace) to impregnate your heart's energy with the sacred vibration.
5. Draw the energy upward to your throat chakra. Breathe in. Exhale.

6. Visualize the energy moving to your third eye. Gaze there and broadcast a call from your soul to the Divine for what you desire—keep the message succinct and clear.
7. Trust and feel confident. Express gratitude for the answer to your request.

HOPE FOR THE LONG VISIT

The archetypal visitor who comes calling is an ancient theme that repeats in every generation. Those who expect visitors have always harbored the hope and expectation that the guest will arrive safely but perhaps entertained the occasional niggling doubt that something could happen. This little doubt is not exactly what it appears to be. It finds resonance in the fact that our very existence on this earth is a visit. When you live a responsible and compassionate life of humility and gratitude, ever aware of the impermanence of all things, as Buddhism teaches, you more easily unknot the fetters that bind you to attachments—the causes of suffering. Some positive reasons to cultivate detachment include:

* You let go of expectations.
* You see things as they are without judging them.
* You let life happen without trying to control the way it happens or the direction.
* You relish happiness but don't cling to it.
* You enjoy the experiences of life more without the attachment.

1. Find a comfortable meditation spot, tune everything out, and turn within.
2. Draw your mind inward and concentrate on the subtle, imperishable One.
3. Know that your true nature is bliss—this is the source of your true happiness. Accept this You.
4. Dive deeply into this wellspring of bliss, for in this happiness you experience your true nature.

HOLD ON TO YOUR HOPES AND DREAMS

The late Steve Jobs said that time is limited and we should not waste it living someone else's life, nor should we be trapped by the dogma of other people's thinking—our own thoughts drowned out by theirs. Your dream is yours. Don't give others the power to push you into abandoning it. That dream is your treasure. If you hope to make it come true, then own that. Get to work manifesting that dream through the power of intention, positive thinking and feeling, affirmations, visualizations, and gratitude for the blessings you already have in your life. Since, as Jobs noted, we have limited time, now would be the moment to start.

1. Write out your dream on a piece of self-stick paper. Place this note in a location where you will see it often, to keep reminding you of what it is calling you to do.
2. Meditate on God, aligning your thoughts with Divine Consciousness and your will with Divine Will.
3. Use pranayama to slow your thoughts and induce inner tranquility.
4. Declare your intention. Focus on your dream and know that it is possible and it is yours to have. Already, your intention is stirring the field of infinite potential and drawing itself into manifestation.
5. Use affirmation or visualization (or both) to reinforce your hope of having that dream come into your world.
6. Abolish all doubt and feel confidently expectant.
7. Thank the Divine Power, which makes all things possible.

MEDITATIONS ON JUSTICE

Think of justice as the application of fairness to protect rights and penalize for wrongdoing. Ancient biblical justice demanded an eye for an eye. During the medieval period, the Hand of Justice staff along with the royal scepter and the crown symbolized the absolute power of European monarchs. In the modern era, leaders such as Gandhi advocated civil disobedience to injustice and preached satyagraha (holding onto truth). Embracing Gandhi's nonviolent princples, Dr. Martin Luther King Jr. preached that only light can dispel darkness.

MINDFULNESS FOR SOCIAL AND CULTURAL JUSTICE

"Justice . . . is the ligament which holds civilized beings and civilized nations together," said nineteenth-century statesman Daniel Webster. In this complex world, there are many categories of justice, including one for which mindfulness can play a key role. Social justice emphasizes a societal/spiritual approach to justice. It requires you to train yourself in patient self-awareness, thoughtfulness, deep introspection, and compassion. Programs that teach social justice look for ways to integrate the necessities of social and cultural justice with mindfulness. Although such work can be done in groups, success depends on individuals in communities across America and throughout the world. It is paramount to understand who you truly are and to be ever mindful of treading the fair and compassionate path to support spiritually informed justice when working for justice for all.

1. Meditate on the spark of the Divine residing in the heart of all humans regardless of color, gender, race, and religious or spiritual preferences.
2. Consider the biases in our society. How different would your life be if you were a different race, for example? What, if any, difference might it make in your life in the realms of justice, economics, and job opportunities?
3. Let your mind wrap around how injustice can teach you about who you want to be, how you want to live your life, and how you want to help others.

KARMIC JUSTICE

The Christian Bible states that you will reap whatever you sow. Eastern wisdom proffers another version of this in karma, the law of consequence—action and reaction. You are being affected by karma every moment of your life; everyone is. Your thoughts, words, and deeds are imbued with an energy that is always dynamic and moving. Karma is that energy. If you want happiness, you can sow seeds for that. Violate the laws of nature (such as by neglecting self-care) and illness shows up. It's a shift and quality change in the energy. Buddhism allows individual maleficent and beneficent conditions to influence how karmic effect is hindered or arises. You, by your volition, create favorable environments and conditions for karma. You may have heard people refer to "good" and "bad" karma, but these are only perceptions. In truth, karma is neither good nor bad; it's just energy.

1. Sit with closed eyes and breathe slowly.
2. Focus on the third-eye (Ajna) chakra and visualize the sacred light of your soul.
3. Analyze your tendency toward routine behaviors and actions; consider their root causes.
4. Imagine a God basket, bucket, or box into which you would place any biases or ingrained behaviors that you no longer want to express. Visualize writing them on paper and dropping the pieces of paper in. When finished, mentally set the basket on the altar of your heart.
5. Run a stream of cleansing, creative light through your chakras; return the light to your heart.
6. Surround the basket in that holy light and release it to the Highest Power.

THE TAROT'S JUSTICE CARD

The Justice card in the tarot depicts Lady Justice as a crowned, robed figure seated between two pillars holding a scale and a sword. Any psychic reading would first weigh the symbolism—the sword held in the right hand indicates action and reason. The sword has a double edge that promises impartiality (it cuts on either side). Lady Justice's left hand (the side of intuition) holds a scale, suggestive of measured judgment. The two pillars symbolize balance; the red robe represents power. The white shoe she wears points to the presence of spiritual power, but it isn't flaunted. The crown projects a disciplined mind. The law of justice is both karmic and spiritual. Use this card as a visualization tool for meditation when you must deal with issues of judgment and fairness.

1. Assume a sitting position of authority in a chair or on the floor.
2. Bring your attention to your throat chakra and visualize blue energy.
3. Listen for the inner sound vibrating "ham."
4. Stay anchored in the here and now as you become saturated in the vibration of the blue energy and sound. The throat chakra is your center for courage.
5. Visualize that tarot Justice card and consider that the sword of meditation cuts through the knot of egoism. What needs to be done to eliminate bias and bring balance?
6. Next, consider the power of your thoughts to transform so that you represent the best qualities as symbolized by Lady Justice.

DISTRIBUTIVE JUSTICE

All creatures in the cosmos have a purpose for being, and Divine Will makes possible what is needed through spiritual laws, such as the laws of potential, attraction, and intention. Karmic retribution or apportionment, when judged to be bad or good, is a matter of perspective and bias, whether you are an individual or belong to a particular group. If there is an imbalance in what you need for your life purpose, clear your chakra energy, do self-introspection and adjustment, and engage in more meditation and good works.

1. Do yoga in a sequence of moves to energize each of your chakras. For example, begin your yoga session for the seven main chakras by doing the Mountain Pose (Tadasana) for the Muladhara chakra. Move into the Wide-Stance Forward Bend (Prasarita Padottanasana) to stimulate the Svadhistana chakra. Segue into the Full Boat Pose (Paripurna Navasana) for the Manipura chakra. The Camel Pose (Ustrasana) is a good one to open the Anahata (heart) chakra. Do the Cobra Pose (Bhujangasana) for the Vishuddha chakra, the Child's Pose (Balasana) for the Ajna (third eye), and the Plow (Halasana) to stimulate the crown chakra. Take your time as you do each pose correctly so that you gain maximum benefit as you energize and rebalance each chakra, in turn.

2. Sit in a comfortable position with a straight spine.

3. Practice mindfulness.

4. Focus your thought on your life's purpose. Do you see an imbalance—an abundance or lack—in what you need to achieve your goal?

5. Imagine a violet color within as you gaze at the third-eye center. Violet is believed to be a transmuting color that eases karmic debt and burden.

6. Consider your Divine Purpose as you see it. Focus on exactly what work you might do to move into accord with the law of distributive justice.

The Path of Nonviolence

When the Standing Rock Sioux tribe in North Dakota believed that the greater good would be served if an oil pipeline were not placed under the Missouri River, tribe members protested in nonviolent resistance. Many people and other tribes stood with these defenders and protectors of water and earth.

JUSTICE AND MORAL LAW

Humanity, in general, subscribes to the idea of moral law as universal. This means adhering to principles of "right" conduct by following moral values of decency and goodness. Adhering to ethical standards garners you a pristine reputation, presents you as a fair and compassionate person, and blesses you with opportunities and good karma. Whether you make an implicit or explicit moral decision, chances are you intend to do the proper or "right" thing. To empower your voice to speak your highest truth about upholding moral standards, start by energizing and healing your throat chakra (Vishuddha). This meditation is especially powerful if you have ever felt your voice silenced.

1. Sit for meditation and bring your focus to the throat chakra.
2. Breathe slowly and rhythmically the So'Ham pattern while keeping your awareness on the throat, mouth, tongue, and larynx.
3. Feel a warm energy flowing there; visualize blue light.
4. Visualize anyone who may have ever silenced or disempowered you and declare what you want to say to him or her (for pranic healing).
5. On exhalations, forgive that person and release all emotional energy that you may have been carrying.
6. Breathe in while meditating on the positive affirmation: "My voice has power, beauty, and worth. My words have value. I speak my highest truth with kindness toward all."
7. Mentally voice other empowering affirmations on inhalation and breathe out what you are no longer willing to harbor.

AHIMSA IN TIMES OF INJUSTICE

The Yoga Aphorisms of Patanjali delineates guidelines for the practice of nonviolence (*ahimsa,* which means non-injury). You are practicing ahimsa when you do not hurt another with your words or actions or even in your thoughts. Ahimsa is a key virtue with no ideas of superiority over others or feeling/showing contempt. Create an environment of ahimsa within your being so that you feel empathy, compassion, and mercy. When you see an injustice, let it call you instantly to right action in thought, word, and deed. Do your favorite meditation technique to feel grounded as you prepare to attune yourself to powerful energies of justice while considering what you will do when or if you experience the following:

1. Notice ill treatment of someone holding a sign that says, "Will work for food."
2. Observe someone kicking a dog.
3. See someone pushing others out of the way to get to the head of a line.
4. Hear someone scream that a thief has snatched her purse.
5. See an act of vandalism in progress.
6. Overhear someone loudly criticizing a competitor or tarnishing someone's reputation.

SOCIAL JUSTICE—SERVING FROM THE INSIDE OUT

In Eastern wisdom traditions the word *seva* means selfless service. To paraphrase a passage in the *The Bhagavad-Gita*, service is defined as that which is performed without consideration of return at the right time and place by someone who considers it his or her duty. Service in such instances is considered moral goodness. Where justice is denied, there are often service organizations to work to correct that wrong. Amnesty International, for example, is a well-known champion of human rights and works to rectify social injustice around the world. Get in touch with your heart chakra, where compassion and love and moral certitude lead you to *seva* in some realm that serves social justice.

1. Turn within and put your attention at the heart center (Anahata).
2. Call upon your Higher Self for the inspiration of where, how, and whom to serve. For example, will you work for environmental justice, awareness of climate change, threats to public lands, endangered species, or ocean pollution issues or to achieve social justice for the most vulnerable in the world or your community?
3. Take time when you leave your yoga mat and meditation to do your due diligence. Read, research, and pinpoint the work and the organization you wish to join. Put together an action plan and a timeline.

SAFEGUARDING WOMEN'S RIGHTS

American women have advanced gender-based causes with success—the right to vote, to own property, to have an equal opportunity to education, to have control over their reproductive rights, and to marry whomever they love. Advocates for women's rights claim that while these are incredible breakthroughs for women, they can erode without vigilance. In America, women serve many roles—wives and mothers, healers, artists, business and political leaders, pioneers, philosophers, and spiritual teachers. These are a few of the areas in which women have broken glass ceilings that previously have limited their reach and power. But in many countries, women still struggle for basic rights. There remains much work to be done. In this arena, too, mindfulness matters.

1. Choose an image of the Divine Feminine or a lotus, a lily, or another flower as a "feminine" meditation focus.
2. Seat yourself in your favorite pose. Gaze at the picture, icon, or statue for a few minutes. Close your eyes and visualize the image at the third-eye chakra (the goal is to see the image in your interiority and to feel unconditional love, *prema,* for the Divine Mother).
3. Chant *OM* or your mantra and let feelings of devotional love (*bhakti*) lead you deeper into the silence within.
4. Immerse yourself in that blissful inner world where there is only awareness without boundary or ceiling.

ACTIVISM AND JUSTICE FOR ANIMAL RIGHTS

Animals have a right to their lives and to not suffer—that assumption underlies the work of many animal rights advocates who attain justice for dogs, cats, chickens, birds, goats, monkeys, and other non-human species. The Buddha taught, "When a man has pity on all living creatures, then only is he noble." Furthermore, the Buddha said that people should discover what their work is and then, with all their heart, give themselves to it. That's what animal rights activists do. For many, this is their life. If such work speaks to your heart, rally around an animal rights cause. And, by all means, forge a deeper bond with the pets in your life.

1. Sit with your pet. Close your eyes and breathe in and out in a slow, smooth rhythm.
2. Anchor yourself in the here and now. Be attentive to your pet. Animal behaviorists say cats will purr contentedly and gaze upon you with a short blink (cat kiss), or wrap or lay their tails on you; dogs may give you sloppy kisses and snuggle next to you.
3. Sink into the rapture of peace and radiate love from your heart into the space around you and your pet.
4. Telepathically send love to your pet (animals have no sense of past or future; they live in the present). When you are fully present to the moment and your pet is, too, you can connect on a deeply intuitive level.

MEDITATIONS ON BIRTH AND DEATH

At birth, breath starts you on the journey of life. At the end of your life, a final breath separates you from death. Tibetan Buddhists believe that human birth presents precious opportunities for spiritual evolution and that spiritual practitioners who realize that life is short may choose to embrace living in a meaningful way. When death comes, as it certainly will, it is not to be feared because your spiritual practices will have introduced you to the inner worlds through which you arrived and someday will depart.

WHY WAIT TO CONTACT THE DIVINE?

From your physical birth, you have had an infinite power to transform everything in your life, just as did your parents, your ancestors, and all sentient beings. All that is required is to open your heart and believe in yourself. There are no fences separating you from the Divine. Some people think they will meet God when they die, but why wait? Turn within, and send out your soul call to the Divine. Tell the Holy One to hurry, hurry. You are waiting. It is the destiny of all of us to evolve and become enlightened.

1. Sit with eyes closed. Focus on your relaxed, regular breathing.
2. Look at your third eye. Imagine that it reflects back to you space stretching out from you into the world, out beyond the atmosphere of earth into deep space, into infinity.
3. Imagine that Divine Love permeates everything and that it is the true love expressed to you through the hearts of your parents and all who care for you.

All Your Ancestors Are Present

Buddhist monk Thich Nhat Hanh counseled, "If you look deeply into the palm of your hand you will see your parents and all generations of your ancestors. All of them are alive in this moment. Each is present in your body. You are the continuation of each of these people."

THE DOORWAY TO THE BEYOND

People who've had near-death experiences report that awareness continues in that gap between death and when bodily functions are restored (when they are brought back to life through interventions). More than that, the awareness becomes expansive. Peace increases. Space becomes limitless. They feel accepted and loved. Many speak of the awareness of a significant presence as the sense of self is swallowed by a magnificent manifestation of a being of light—the eternal Self. As in death, meditation can take you to that presence—in your heart. With meditative practice, you can awaken to the spaciousness and lightness of being, complete acceptance, and peace. Saints and sages of many traditions say death is no more than a doorway with a threshold you've crossed countless times.

1. Sit in the cross-legged position of the Lotus or Half Lotus. Focus your awareness on your breath.
2. Count the number on exhalation and "God" or another word you hold as sacred on inhalation.
3. Turn your awareness to the heart. Enter in. Feel the vibration. Listen for the sound of "Yam" (like "lama"). See soft green light—nurturing and healing—filling the space. It flows through and around you until there is nothing that is not permeated by that gentle light.
4. Imagine that your consciousness expands into the space and awareness of your body falls away.
5. Rest in conscious awareness of ever-expanding space, light, and peace. Death can't touch you there.

THE CESSATION OF BREATH ALSO SYMBOLIZES BIRTH

On his last day on earth, Buddha became sick after his final meal. Still, he managed to teach, accept a last disciple, and ask his monks if they had any doubts or questions. None did. With equanimity, poise, and grace, he accepted the inevitable. He taught that only after you pass from life and death is there blissful peace. There is nothing to fear. Like a bird freed from a cage, you leave your body behind to soar—your soul knows how to go home.

1. Prepare for death by living your life as though any moment might be your last.
2. Carry on your life's work without attachment to the fruits of your labor or objects of the senses. Free yourself of encumbrances. Practice loving-kindness and compassion toward all.
3. Realize the impermanence of life and all things.
4. Accept what comes into your life with grace and dignity. You are only here for a short time.
5. Begin a sadhana (personal spiritual practice). Meditate often; it prepares you.
6. Do not fear, but remain absorbed in meditation.

Vesak

Theravada and the Tibetan Buddhists combine the events of the Buddha's birth and death and enlightenment into a single celebratory day known as Vesak.

PAST-LIFE REGRESSION AS A HEALING MODALITY

Increasingly, healers are turning to hypnotic past-life regression to ease their patients' physical and emotional suffering in this life. In this healing modality, your phobia or anxiety disappears when you can recall the past life in which the issue originated. You remain aware as your thoughts take you ever deeper into a super relaxed state. Hypnosis enhances your memory through focused concentration; it's safe to stop and open your eyes. Although self-hypnosis has been deemed safe by doctors, psychologists, and others in the medical profession, if you become uncomfortable with the practice simply stop the process by opening your eyes.

1. Wear loose clothes. Sit in a chair and close your eyes. Lower the lights and listen to soft instrumental music.
2. Exhale tension. Inhale. See radiant light around you.
3. Relax your face muscles, jaw, neck, and shoulders. Exhale and feel the warmth of healing.
4. Relax every part of your body.
5. Visualize the light entering your crown, flowing down and up your spine, and spreading throughout your body.
6. Exhale. Descend deeper. Face a doorway with a beautiful numinous light beyond.
7. Step through. Enter the light. Let go of body awareness. Open yourself to all your memories. Glide further into your awareness. Go to an early childhood memory.
8. Notice everything—what do you see? How do you feel? Who is with you? What's happening?

9. Feel deeply relaxed, healed, and safe. There's no death and dying here. You have existed forever as an eternal soul.
10. Count backward slowly from ten. Feel all dimensions of yourself completely nourished, healed, and at peace. Resting in awareness, remember all that you have experienced.

MENTAL IMPULSE INFORMS THE DESIRE TO CREATE STUFF

Germination begins with conception. In the plant world, germination takes place in the earth, deep underground in the darkness. When a plant reaches a certain stage of maturity, it pushes through the soil to emerge into the light, where photosynthesis helps it to mature further and fulfill its purpose. Buddhism uses a term that finds resonance in the idea of germination—*cetana,* or the mental impulses associated with actualizing something. For example, you are a builder with the intention to build a shed. You direct your crew (the carpenter, mason, electrician, plumber, and roofer) to get on it. Thanks to your initial mental impulse, you now have a shed. Eastern wisdom traditions teach that cetana binds you to endless cycles of birth and death. Awareness of how cetana constantly pulls you into manifesting things means you can decide to not yield to mental impulses.

1. Draw your senses inward, away from the wild world.
2. Tuck your tongue up against the back of your upper teeth.
3. Inhale through your nose and mentally count to four. Hold your breath as you mentally count to seven. Exhale through your mouth around your tongue to the count of seven.
4. Do this three times. Breathe naturally; feel the energy in your head.
5. Observe the thoughts that arise and release them.
6. Put your mind on your breath if thoughts become active and strong. Remember that you control the body, not the other way around.

THOUSANDS OF SPARKS

In the Mundaka Upanishad, there is a description of the Creator (symbolized as a flame) causing thousands of sparks to come into being. These sparks are humans—an infinity of them—who, after living out their lives, will return to their source, the Creator. The passage goes on to say that beyond the Creator is the eternal spirit of light that is within all. Some might take comfort in the idea that the passage must mean by the grace of God, the spark of the Divine is within everyone. The naysayers might then point out that it isn't possible for God to dwell within if there is no inside or outside. All beings and bits of creation constitute a collective whole. When your consciousness has drowned into the infinite cosmic consciousness, there is no longer the perception of duality but rather oneness with all things.

1. Do your favorite breath work for a few minutes.
2. Sit in a comfortable pose. Turn within and place your awareness at the third-eye or Ajna chakra, the center of wisdom, imagination, and intuition.
3. Focus deeply on the inner sound of thousands of tinkling bells associated with this chakra.
4. Let that sound take you deeper within realms that have not yet revealed themselves.
5. Reflect on examples of duality thinking, and then consider how duality ends when the individual self (*jiva-atman*) merges into the Supreme Soul (*Paramatman*). This is the transcendent goal of the spiritual aspirant.

TAP INTO THE REGENERATIVE POWER OF SCORPIO

One of the twelve signs of the zodiac, Scorpio is the notable sign of regeneration. This astrological sign is associated with decay, the underworld, and that which is hidden from view—secrets. Pluto rules the sign. In Classical mythology, Pluto is the Lord of the Underworld and oversees death, rebirth, and regeneration. Scorpio signals death, change, and transformation. Scorpios are often good at perceiving what is hidden. Whatever change comes careening into their lives, they land on their feet. Put Scorpio's special powers to work for you. When imbalance shows up in the personal, professional, or spiritual area of your life, dare to peek behind the illusory screen to see what elements are hidden from view. You may have to reimagine your job or transform a spiritual endeavor to get back on track, but with Scorpio's power to transform, success is yours to claim.

1. Close your eyes and breathe naturally in a regular rhythmic pattern.
2. Mentally count your breaths to ten, like so: OM . . . one; OM . . . two; OM . . . three. Completely empty your lungs on the exhaled breath.
3. Put your attention at the heart chakra, long associated with compassion, regeneration, transformation, and empowerment.
4. Visualize a green light in your heart. It emerges, expands, and fills your being to clear away old patterns of thinking and being to facilitate change.
5. Let your inner voice of wisdom guide you. Trust the energy that never dies but transforms.

HEAL OLD WOUNDS TO GENERATE RENEWAL

Mindfulness helps you reset your perspective when a memory of a past traumatic event resurfaces and produces emotional or physical stress. The tension you feel over that memory in the present, according to science, is secondary stress created from your recollection of the pain and suffering you endured when the event first happened. Mindfulness teaches the brain the art of observing the mind's content without trying to fix what's coming up. Whenever you become aware of triggers and thought patterns taking you back to past pain, use mindfulness to draw you back into the present. Your goal is to observe the pain. Realize that it's in the past and can't hurt you now. Let it go and find healing and renewal.

1. Close your eyes. Breathe naturally. Focus on what your senses are experiencing. How are you feeling?
2. Notice how your thoughts and emotions shift when a change occurs in your environment, such as a loud noise or a sound that takes you back to the hurt. How does your body/mind respond when your senses notice a change or trigger in the present for that past trauma?
3. Shift to a controlled breathing pattern, such as inhaling to the count of four and exhaling to the count of six or eight. Does the shift in your breathing pattern (intended to draw you back into the present) also create a change in how you feel?

SUBDUE YOUR MIND WAVES

There exists in every moment of your life an undeniable power for conscious change. Whether you realize it or not, a transformation is always happening. You are not the person you were as a baby or a teen. Your body has undergone significant changes, and your thoughts and perceptions have also matured. Some changes take place over time as you grow and evolve. Others can happen instantaneously—through acts of synchronicity, miraculous cures, the willful touch of an enlightened being, or an act of Grace. On one level, your eternal soul—the essence of who you are—remains unchanged. But on a materialistic and human level, change happens through the action of your mind waves and fine mental impressions. These, you can subdue.

1. Sit with your eyes closed.
2. Visualize the change you desire.
3. Consider what might impede this change and mentally remove all obstacles, such as negative thinking, fear, and doubt—and the *samskaras*, or mental impressions, that give rise to unhelpful ideas. (Patanjali identified "fine samskaras" that can be dissolved in meditation. These samskaras are finer than the mind waves, or chitta vrittis, and the best way to deal with them is to stand sentry at the door of your mind. Get control of these before they become big mental waves pushing you toward choices with negative consequences—for example, self-doubt about doing yoga or spiritual practices that results in inactivity; or, fear of failure that keeps you from challenging yourself to fully express your talents.)
4. State a clear intention for a positive change.

5. Visualize how this change will cause a shift in other areas of your life.
6. Feel joy and anticipation.
7. Count your blessings and feel gratitude for being able to change and craft yourself into the being you want to be.

MEDITATIONS
ON PRESENCE

Who better to reflect back to you the warmth of a loving presence if not your dearest friend? There are many beautiful expressions of the intimate relationship of best friends in faith traditions of the world—past and present. For example, "soul mates" here in America finds resonance in the Buddhist term of "kalyana-mitra" (spiritual, noble, or admirable friend). The ancient Celts called a soul friend, "anam cara." Regardless of the words you use for your soul friend, cherish him or her for fulfilling that primal longing in every human heart—the need for presence.

NOTICE THE PRESENCES IN YOUR LIFE

When you are looking forward in anticipation of what the future holds or gazing back in time wishing to recapture or rewrite chapters in your life's story, you are missing the presences of beings (seen and unseen) in the moment. Notice and feel gratitude for the presence of those walking this journey of life alongside you, both outwardly (friends, family, mentors, pets, coworkers, and fellow students) and inwardly (the lineage of spiritual teachers, saints and sacred helpers, angels, and protectors). If you have loved ones who are far from home, speak to them as though they are near (you are already holding them in intimacy in your heart). For loved ones who have passed away, take the time to send a blessing of love to them. Smile and feel gratitude when thoughts of them pop up during your day as if to say, "Hey, I'm here."

1. Enter into silence.
2. Breathe in for four counts, hold for four counts, breathe out for eight counts, and hold for four counts.
3. Continue the controlled breathing.
4. Plunge deeper into meditation.
5. Call upon the presence of your guru or spiritual teacher and attune yourself to his or her energy.
6. Make a promise to yourself and your teacher to cultivate awareness to the presences in your life.
7. Insert your intention into the field of infinite potential during "hold" counts.
8. Let go and trust that your message has been received.
9. Breathe normally. Rest and feel gratitude.

meditation 2

LET MUSIC LIFT YOU INTO SACRED PRESENCE

To find peace amid the stresses of modern life take refuge in silence, where you find peace in sacred presence. A lovely way to enter is to listen to some beautiful music.

1. Sit in a relaxed position, close your eyes, and tune in to your heart.
2. Listen with a deep awareness to your musical selection. If you don't have a piece of music in mind, try Samuel Barber's "Adagio for Strings" (while imaging the soul's climb to enlightenment). The piece, noted for its emotional intensity, poetic gentleness, and great gasp at its climax (when all the music fades into complete silence for a moment), was first performed in 1938 after the Great Depression and as the world lurched toward war.
3. Take note of the diverse instruments, the rhythm, the minor and major chords, the fingering of stringed instruments, the backbeats of drums, and the overall energy vibration and feelings that come from your heart.
4. Notice what happens to your awareness when the musical cadences and tonal patterns change.
5. Observe how when a single instrument plays an important passage, it intensifies your emotional response.
6. Pay attention to what you experience in your heart center when the music reaches the climax and drops away.
7. During the final strains, notice how the emotion in your heart is lifted and opened as the sublime music speaks to a higher presence—your eternal Soul.

KINDLE THE LIGHTS

Whether symbolic, ceremonial, or as a manifestation of the Sacred, many religions of the world light candles in their services. Light illuminates; it enlightens. It protects you against spiritual darkness. Candlelight infuses an atmosphere with tranquility. It's the reason you might light a candle before your bath to soak away the cares of your day, or switch on a soft light as you prepare for bed. If you keep a space in your home where you say prayers or meditate, place a candle there to light. The flame calls you inward and beckons the Holy One to draw near.

1. Light your candle and pray, "May this symbol of light and joy illuminate my path, kindle spiritual knowledge within me, and burn away the dross of false thinking." Sit straight and quiet. Say a prayer or recite a mantra as an invitation to the presence you desire to bless you.
2. Be still, quiet, and psychically attuned to presence in the space around you.
3. Notice the scent of the space, even if it is faint. The fragrance of roses has long been associated with Mary, Mother of God. Through time, devotees of certain powerful Indian gurus have described smelling a pleasing incense fragrance when their master drew near.
4. Sink into the embrace of belonging.

meditation 4

USE IMAGERY TO FIND PRESENCE

In Tibetan Buddhist temples in Nepal and India, you may see bells, drums, and often an elaborate Buddha (sometimes covered in gilt). Exquisite mandalas (geometric designs with spiritual meanings) and thangka scrolls (religious art that traces back to ancient India) adorn the walls. In the privacy of your home sanctuary, use spiritual or religious imagery not as an object to worship but as a bridge to lead you inward into Holy Presence.

1. Find a piece of religious imagery for which you feel an attraction. It might be an image in a book, a photo of something in a temple that spoke to you, or a small Buddha statue you found in a shop. Place it where you can see it.

2. Play a CD of devotional music such as Hindu bhajans, quiet New Age instrumentals, or Buddhist meditation music (with or without chants). Light incense and a candle.

3. Sit in a comfortable position in a chair where you can look at the image.

4. Soak up as many details as possible as you gaze at the picture. Catholic tradition has a devotional hour when you can sit and silently spend time gazing upon the Christ or his mother, Mary. When your mind tires, turn your attention to the music, scent, or candle flame, and then return your focus to the image

5. Close your eyes and check in at your heart center. Feel how the unseen flow of energy out to the picture and back connects you to a sense of peace and presence.

FIND ANCIENT PRESENCE IN CENTURIES-OLD SANCTUARIES

If you find it spiritually uplifting to visit temples, churches, caves, and holy sites in the world, you'll appreciate the exquisite iconostases (the partitions on which icons are mounted) in Russian and Greek Eastern Orthodox churches. The icons and paintings are windows to the sacred. Centuries of veneration imbue these iconostases with an almost palpable energy. In Roman Catholic churches in the United States and abroad—from small towns to cities with soaring cathedrals—you'll find stunning stained glass, statues, and holy objects of veneration. There are Buddhist and Hindu temples across America that will welcome you into their spiritual sanctuaries. The spiritual energy in many holy places can be subtle or electrically charged by the devotional practice of those who chant, pray, and/or meditate there. The energy calls for the presence of the sacred in all and benefits everyone.

1. Join others in a group meditation session.
2. Show your deep regard for the practice and respect for the organization's established rules by doing your best not to be intrusive. Be respectful in your attire, your manners, interactions with others, and entering and leaving.
3. Join in the singing or chanting and dive deeply into your meditation when the time comes.
4. Visualize the presence of your meditation master or beings in your spiritual lineage. Feel them blessing you.
5. Let the devotion in your heart grow to fill you and the room.
6. Deeply dive into that super-charged energy and allow it to carry you into ever-higher (or deeper) realms of consciousness.

THE LANDSCAPE OF LONGING

You retain a strong connection to the site of your final goodbye to someone whom you deeply loved. It's as though the landscape itself held the heart energy of your beloved. It's the place that gives comfort to you when you need to feel that presence again. Your heart energy of belonging to each other remains there, where you secretly gather for old times' sake on the anniversary of the ending or whenever love draws you back. The place might be a sweeping mountaintop, the shoreline of a great sea, a cemetery of moss-covered stones and silhouetted angels, a garden populated with flowers and trees, or a field where the winter wheat waves tall under an endless sky. Wherever your special landscape is, enter into an embrace of belonging there and let your mortal love call you toward the Source of all love.

1. Go to your special place of memory. Wrap yourself in a blanket or shawl against any chill.
2. Find a safe place to sit cross-legged with palms up and open on your thighs.
3. Close your eyes. Breathe out. Send out your heart song or soul call. Breathe in. Receive the presence of your soul friend.
4. Notice how your heart fills with tender feelings as private and deeply personal memories come flooding back.
5. Visualize that spiritual being of light approaching. Send forth your love as a blessing. Receive all the love meant for you. Take it into your heart. Be present with all that there is for you there. Then turn your thoughts to the Holy One's presence, which made love arise in you.

REMEMBERING THE PRESENCE OF ANCESTORS

Ancestor veneration to honor deeds and memories of not only family members but also ancient heroes, beloved saints, esteemed sages, or one's line of gurus is an important aspect of Tibetan Buddhism, Hinduism, Catholicism, and Taoism, among other faiths and practices. In some traditions, you can attend family celebrations that are low-key and reverent. Others launch large festivals. In the three-day Día de los Muertos (Day of the Dead) celebration in Mexico, the spirits of children who have died are invited to visit the altar the children have constructed. On the second day, the spirits of deceased adults are welcomed. Then, on the following day, known as All Souls Day, the family carries decorations to the cemetery. If you'd like to invite the presences of those who have passed on, create a tradition that you feel honors them and venerate them at least once a year.

1. Cover a table with fresh flowers, water, incense, and a candle. Add a picture of the deceased along with a favorite object that would have been permeated with his or her energy—a pocket watch, a locket, a swatch of hair, or a wedding band, for example.
2. Kneel before the table and light the candle and incense. In Taoism, the joss stick or incense is lit and the smoke carries the communication to the ancestor.
3. Make the ceremony yours with traditions you create. For example, set out a bowl of the popcorn he was always so crazy about. Or, arrange sliced oranges on her favorite plate.
4. Dive deep into stillness. Invite him, her, or them to come. Enjoy their presence.

SIT WITH A TREE

In Northern California's Humboldt County, which extends almost to the Oregon border, an ancient forest shelters biologically diverse and rare species of plants and animals—some endangered. When you walk in this forest, you feel inconsequential. These towering old trees stretch toward infinity even as they stand in community with each other along with saplings, dead trees, and fossils that date back millions of years. Standing in an old-growth forest calls to your senses. It's easy to feel a presence there. These living, silent sentinels know the secrets of ancient times. Let your spirit be sheltered by the indwelling presence of an old tree that holds the mysteries and secrets of its life in rings, silent and invisible.

1. Seek out a tree. Spread out a blanket and do a favorite yoga sequence. Rest and focus on the tree's bark and canopy, noticing details.
2. Observe the bark, diameter, and height of the trunk, as well as the branching pattern and the leaves.
3. Close your eyes. Feel the energy of sap moving from the dark roots, up the trunk, and throughout the tree, providing it sustenance. Enjoy the tree's sheltering presence.
4. Imagine your consciousness is in that sap. Feel the flow as though your spirit and the tree are merging into one consciousness. Reimagine the time spent with the tree in other moments of your life when you aren't able to spring free and escape into nature.

THE MEMORY OF PLACE

Find the image of the Divine in the wild and beautiful landscapes of the world. Let your eyes alight upon a flower-draped meadow, red cliffs, a deep and silent spring, lavender hills at sunset, or a swift-flowing river rushing along an ancient course from its source to the sea. This natural beauty has existed in stillness since time immemorial. When you are ready to experience the Divine in a particular place, go there and instead of closing off your senses, open them and your heart to the blessings of presence and the memory of place. Imprinting the images will help you recall them later for a relaxing meditation on peace and well-being.

1. Stand where you can take in a spectacular sunset or moonrise or a landscape that fills your being with awe and wonder.
2. Practice mindfulness, taking in every sensation.
3. Imprint each sensation in your mind: "I smell dust and olive blossom and sun-scorched earth. I hear the screech of a seabird, the rat-a-tat-tat of a woodpecker, the territorial hoot of an owl. I taste the salt of sea air. The breeze kisses my skin with its cool breath as it blows down the mountain."
4. Feel the Divine Presence permeating the landscape, the air, and you. Let go of ego consciousness as the "perceiver" and merge with that Oneness.

INDEX

Abundance, 48, 50, 84, 141
Affirmations
  for abundance, 50
  benefits of, 103
  for friendships, 67
  for gratitude, 51, 65
  for guidance, 112
  for healing, 128
  for hope, 129, 135
  for humanitarian work, 90
  for humility, 116, 119, 124
  for intention, 37, 70
  for justice, 143
  for love, 65, 70, 73, 75–77
  for mercy, 96, 102
  for peace, 28, 129
  for relationships, 67
  for relaxation, 129
  for self-love, 75–77
  for self-mercy, 96
  for synchronicity, 50
  transmitting, 26
  for willpower, 37
Ahimsa, 62, 144
Altruism, 107
Ancestors, 88, 150, 168
Anger, releasing, 35, 96
Animal rights, 79, 147
Animals, love for, 62, 65, 147
Apology, 52, 93, 98–99, 119. See also Forgiveness
Aromatherapy, 76
Attraction, law of, 38

Balance, restoring, 9–10, 23, 28, 33–34, 78, 120

Birth, 149–50, 152, 155
Breath control, 12–15, 55, 78, 128, 135

Camel Pose, 58, 141
Candles, lighting, 121, 164–65, 168
Career, 39, 78, 109, 118
Chakras, 12–14, 23
Challenges, 43, 51, 159
Chants, 15–16, 24, 27, 38. See also Mantras
Child's Pose, 40, 56, 58, 107, 141
Clarity
  hope and, 125, 127, 129
  of life purpose, 47
  mindfulness for, 103
  positive thinking for, 64
  for special causes, 79
  willpower and, 31, 39
Cobra Pose, 74, 141
Coincidences, 47, 54
Community, 79, 105, 113, 145
Compassion, 62–63, 69–79, 89–94, 104. See also Kindness
Competitors, 121
Consequence, law of, 139
Control, relinquishing, 32
Corpse Pose, 20, 96
Courage, 22, 36, 86, 91, 94
Creativity, 10, 13, 46, 50, 88, 155
Crisis, 91, 96–97, 101, 104, 132–33, 158
Cultural connections, 66
Cultural justice, 138. See also Justice

Darkness and light, 63, 95, 126–27, 137, 164

Death
birth and, 149, 152
Divine contact and, 150
Divine spark and, 156
doorway of, 151
fear of, 149, 152
near-death experiences, 151
past-life regression, 153–54
peace and, 151–54
regeneration and, 114, 157
transformation and, 150, 157–60

Decluttering process, 52–53

Desires, manifesting, 38, 155. See also Manifestations

Distress, 101. See also Mercy

Divine, contacting, 150

Divine Guidance, 58

Divine Light, 89

Divine Love, 69–70, 89, 150

Divine Power, 20, 48, 95, 127, 135

Divine qualities, 59

Divine Spark, 62, 156

Divine Will, 28, 48, 112, 135, 141

Doorways, 46, 151, 163

Doubts, 43, 131, 134, 135, 159

Dreams, 25, 54

Earth
blessing, 87
caring for, 42, 61
coexistence with, 20
energy of, 20
mindfulness for, 61
nature and, 20, 21, 42, 61, 82, 87, 114, 169
peace with, 20, 21
renewal of, 131
seasons of, 114, 131

Ego, 94–95, 112, 115, 119, 170

Emotional baggage, 52

Emotions, redirecting, 35

Empathy, 60, 75, 94, 107, 110, 144

Environmental justice, 145. See also Justice

Focus, benefits of, 11, 14, 31. See also Mindfulness

Foot washing, 122. See also Humility

Forgiveness, 52, 93–104, 119

Fortune, 84, 123

Friendliness, 63, 66

Friendship, 57–67, 85

Full Boat Pose, 141

Germination, 155

Gifts, 71, 82, 84, 114, 116

Gratitude, 51, 65, 77, 81–91

Gratitude journal, 83

Guidance, 49, 55, 58, 109, 112

Happiness
friendliness and, 63, 66
gratitude and, 82–86
hope and, 126, 134
humility and, 121
joy and, 19, 38, 82–86, 164
karma and, 139
measuring, 50
peace and, 73
relaxation and, 29
self-acceptance and, 134

Harmony, 33–34, 47, 113, 117, 120

Healing
affirmation for, 128
aromatherapy and, 76
energies from, 12, 20, 89
forgiveness and, 95
friendliness and, 63
holistic healing, 29
hope and, 128
mantra for, 15

moral law and, 143
for old wounds, 158
past-life regression and,
    153–54
renewal and, 158
sleep and, 54
Heart, opening, 18–19, 58, 65
Hindrances, 43, 159
Hope, 125–35
Humanitarian work, 90
Humility, 115–24

Imagery, 12, 36, 103, 165
Imagination, 13, 88
Infinite, doorway to, 46
Infinite possibilities, 39, 46–48,
    54
Injustice, 104, 137–38, 144–45
Intention, 31–43, 45–48, 70–72,
    82, 135
Interconnectedness, 47, 49, 61,
    66, 74, 86, 94

Journal of gratitude, 83. See also
    Gratitude
Joy, 19, 38, 82–86, 164. See also
    Happiness
Justice
    affirmation for, 143
    animal rights and, 79, 147
    biblical justice, 137
    cultural justice, 138
    distributive justice, 141–42
    environmental justice, 145
    injustice and, 104, 137–38,
        144–45
    karmic justice, 139–43
    law of, 139–40, 142
    mindfulness for, 138
    moral law and, 143
    social justice, 138, 145
    Tarot cards and, 140

Karma, 118, 139–43
Karmic fate, 129, 139–42
Karmic justice, 139–43
Kindness, 19–20, 35, 63–66,
    73–75, 93–99, 152. See also
    Compassion
Knots symbolism, 74

Life changes, 55, 96, 108–9, 129,
    131, 159
Life purpose, 11, 40–41, 47, 141–42
Light, shining, 63, 89, 121, 126–27,
    137, 164–65, 168
Loss, 91, 96–97, 167–68
Lotus Pose, 100, 103
Love
    affirmations for, 65, 70, 73,
        75–77
    for animals, 62, 65, 147
    aromatherapy and, 76
    circle of, 70
    energy of, 76
    peace and, 26, 73, 147
    for pets, 62, 65, 147
    self-love, 70, 75–78, 98, 110,
        114
    for special causes, 79
    for success, 78
    transmitting, 26
    words for, 77
Loving-kindness, 19–20, 35,
    73–75, 93, 98–99, 152

Manifestations, 38, 46, 126, 135,
    151, 155, 164
Mantras, 13–15, 24, 38, 72, 95,
    126
Meditation benefits, 9–16
Memories, 153, 158, 168–70
Mental clutter, 52–53
Mental impulse, 155
Mercy, 93–97, 101–4

Mindfulness
  benefits of, 103–4, 158
  breathing and, 11, 16
  clarity and, 103
  earth and, 61
  focus and, 11, 14, 31
  for friendships, 60
  humility and, 119
  for justice, 138
  nature and, 21, 61
  practicing, 21, 103–4, 108–9,
    123–24, 128, 141, 170
  prayer and, 119
  redirecting emotions, 35
  renewal and, 158
  willpower and, 33–34
Mind, quieting, 18–19, 27
Mind waves, 94, 129, 159–60
Moral law, 143
Moral values, 62, 67, 143, 145
Mountain Pose, 141
Music, 15–16, 29, 153, 163, 165

Nature, seasons of, 114, 131
Nature walks, 11, 20–21, 42,
  60–61, 82, 169
Near-death experiences, 151. See
  also Death
Negative thoughts, 21, 32, 51–52,
  63, 159
Nonviolence, 20, 42, 62, 142, 144

Obstacles, 43, 159
Oneness, 61, 71, 91, 156, 170

Past-life regression, 153–54
Past, releasing, 158
Peace
  achieving, 17–29
  affirmations for, 28, 129
  chants for, 24, 27
  during crisis, 132–33
  death and, 151–54
  decluttering and, 52–53
  earth and, 20, 21
  eternal peace, 26
  happiness and, 73
  hope and, 127–30
  inner peace, 18–19, 22, 59
  love and, 26, 73, 147
  meditations on, 17–29
  music and, 163
  nature and, 20, 21
  presence and, 163–65
  quiet minds and, 18–19, 27
  reducing stress, 23, 163–65
  relaxation and, 10–11, 48
  serenity and, 10, 19, 82, 118, 129
  silence and, 59, 102, 143, 146,
    162–63
  sleep and, 25
  transmitting, 26
  world peace, 130
  yoga for, 25
Pets, 62, 65, 147
Positive thoughts, 9, 26–32,
  38–39, 64, 95, 110, 135
Praise, 72, 116, 118, 120, 124
Pranama, 123, 126
Pranayama, 12, 14–15, 55, 78, 128,
  135
Prayer beads, 24, 38, 132
Prayers, 16–17, 24, 26, 38, 89, 119,
  164. See also Affirmations;
  Chants
Prayer wheel mantra, 72. See also
  Mantras
Presence
  of ancestors, 168
  experiencing, 161–70
  imagery for, 165
  in landscapes, 167
  of loved ones, 167–68
  memories and, 168–70

music and, 163, 165
   peace and, 163–65
   sacred presence, 163–65
   in sanctuaries, 166
   silence and, 163
   trees and, 169
Prosperity, 48, 109, 123
Psychic energy, 12, 54–56, 103, 140
Purpose of life, 11, 40–41, 47, 141–42

Red lotus, 71
Regeneration, 114, 157
Relationships, 57–67, 85, 100
Relaxation, 10–11, 25, 29, 48, 96–97, 129
Renewal, 59, 131, 157–58
Resolve, 37, 103
Respect, 61, 66, 98, 123, 124, 126, 166

Sacred presence, 163–65. See also Presence
Sacrifice, 105–14
Sanctuaries, 166
Scorpio, 157
Seasons, 114, 131
Self-acceptance, 134
Self-care, 78–79, 110, 139
Self-love, 70, 75–78, 98, 110, 114
Self-mercy, 96–97
Self-realization, 16, 26
Self-respect, 112
Serenity, 10, 19, 82, 118, 129. See also Peace
Silence, 59, 102, 143, 146, 162–63
Singing bowl, 16, 29
Sleep, 25, 54
Social justice, 138, 145. See also Justice
Spark of Divine, 156

Spirit, soothing, 29
Strength, 22, 36, 39, 51, 59
Stress, reducing, 9–11, 23, 158, 163–65
Success, 48, 50, 78, 118–19, 121, 157
Synchronicity, 45–56

Tarot cards, 36, 140
Traumatic events, 91, 96–97, 101, 104, 132–33, 158

Unity, law of, 50
Universe, wisdom of, 48, 55, 94

Vesak, 152
Veterans, 65, 89, 108
Vices, 63, 120
Virtues, 33–34, 63, 73, 91, 116–24, 144
Volunteerism, 79

Walking meditation, 11, 21, 60. See also Nature walks
Warrior Pose, 22
Wealth, 48, 109, 123
Willpower, 31–43
Women rights, 146
Worry, relinquishing, 28, 55
Wounds, healing, 158

Yoga
   benefits of, 9, 11–15, 94
   for peaceful sleep, 25
   practicing, 11–15, 20–27, 50, 75, 107, 117–18, 126
   types of, 11–12

ABOUT THE AUTHOR

Meera Lester, an internationally published author and world traveler, has written nearly thirty books including *Sacred Travels, The Everything® Law of Attraction Book*, and *The Secret Power of You* as well as mysteries. Since spending time in India and Nepal in her early twenties, she has been a devoted practitioner of hatha yoga, dhyana meditation, and kundalini maha yoga.